MY GRACE IS
SUFFICIENT

These brief memories of a special time in our lives are dedicated to Lizzie with whom I have shared so many adventures.

MY GRACE IS SUFFICIENT

The Miracle of Medicine –
Letters from Bangladesh

JULIAN DAVEY

HISTORY INTO PRINT

First published by
History Into Print, 19 Enfield Ind. Estate,
Redditch, Worcestershire B97 6BY in 2023
www.history-into-print.com

ISBN: 978-1-85858-355-6

A Cataloguing in Publication Record
for this title is available from the British Library.

Typeset in Baskerville
Printed in Great Britain by
4edge Ltd.

CONTENTS

Introduction   vii

1.   1973   1

2.   1974   16

3.   1975   82

Postscript   131

"*My grace is sufficient for you, for my power is made perfect in weakness.*"

St. Paul's Second Letter to the Corinthians

INTRODUCTION

I've always known that those few years in Bangladesh had a profound effect on my life. But I had often wondered why, for memories fade and my subsequent life has been busy. It was only when I discovered a large bundle of letters sent home from Bollobhpur that I realised why that brief time had remained so significant.

Of course, correspondence is a two-way process and much happened at home during those two years including my father's illness, my brothers' divorces and the ongoing political crises which gripped the nation in the early 1970s. Not least were my late mother's tireless efforts to draw attention to our work and to keep up a constant supply of packeted foods, newspapers and letters of encouragement. I am deeply grateful to her for safely keeping all my missives so that I could read them at a future date.

To focus on the life that we experienced in Bangladesh with all its ups and downs, triumphs and disasters, I have removed almost all the references as to what was happening at home. But, apart from adding *italics* and heading the paragraphs to make them easier to read, the letters remain essentially the same.

I hope you will find as much enjoyment reading these letters as I had rediscovering them.

JWD, Alcester, 2023

Chapter 1

1973

19 November Tuesday

Dearest Both,

I'm sure you will be relieved to know that I have arrived safely in Bollobhpur. Let me try to give you my first impressions:

I stepped down from the Land Rover and looked around at the hospital where I was going to work for the next two years. In the dusty compound were groups of women and children, bullock carts, chickens and a mangy-looking dog. The English nurses came out to welcome me. "*Isn't he big!*" someone said, no doubt concerned about the future food situation!

Having initially travelled to language school through the Sundarbans to *Barisal* on board the ancient *Rocket* steamship, we then journeyed a further hundred and forty miles north to Bollobhpur by Land Rover, staying at *Khulna* overnight. Fields of golden rice stretched in every direction, with palm, mango and bamboo trees dotted here and there. The narrow road passed through multiple villages, with children on their way to school looking well-fed, healthy and smiling. Cattle were everywhere and chickens flew in every direction. We crossed the final river on a ferry consisting of a bamboo platform strung across two fishing boats, barely wide enough to hold the Land Rover. The last ten miles to Bollobhpur was a rutted and dusty track and I began to realise just how remote this hospital was going to be!

Florence, Meg and Pat, volunteers Lizzie and Eryl, and a young Indian doctor, Benny, had been eating lunch on the veranda at the back of the large mission house which overlooks the river and the fields beyond. A garden full of flowers separated the hospital from the house.

A new bungalow had been built for Benny and myself about eighty yards from the hospital, so I had a welcome rest in the cool of the bungalow before rejoining everyone on the veranda for tea. It was good to have real milk and real bread for the first time in six weeks. Everybody was very friendly and relaxed and there was much talk about my background, my journey and the latest news from England.

That evening, straightaway after dinner, I was thrown in at the deep end! A lady in labour had been admitted and was making little progress, so I found myself doing a difficult forceps delivery by lamplight with Lizzie standing on a stool holding a drip. They have plenty of IV fluids here at the moment, but no drip-stands. Thank goodness there was no problem and the baby was delivered safely.

I'm going to stop writing now. The mosquitoes have begun to bite, it's dark and the hurricane lamp on my table has started to flicker. I'm told that the generator, which provides electricity for the hospital, is working only intermittently since it broke down six weeks ago. Tomorrow morning I'm looking forward to going over to the hospital and starting my work.

26 November

Caesarean Section by Torchlight

My first obstetric emergency happened a couple of nights ago when a young mother presented with a placenta previa requiring an emergency caesarean section, the first one performed in the hospital for five years. Everything here is basic. Eryl anaesthetised the patient with an EMO vaporiser machine – the first time I had seen anyone using ether. The operating light worked for the greater part of the operation, but the generator stopped before I had begun to close and the nurses resorted to using hand-held battery torches. Both mum and babe were OK. We went back to the big house and stayed up late, drinking cups of tea and talking over the experience – such a mixture of excitement and relief.

Let me tell you about the village. Bollobhpur is situated on the banks of the river and consists of thatched houses made of mud and cow dung. Several generations of one family live in individual houses built around each small compound. It's a great time of the year for me to arrive because it feels like a warm June day at home. I am told that the hot months begin after March. All the villagers are friendly, greeting us with *"Nomoska"* and putting their hands together up to their faces. It happens many times a day and we respond in the same way.

Ten miles of rough track and a river separate us from the nearest town, *Meherpur,* where we have another small maternity hospital and an outpatient clinic which is visited on a Wednesday and a Saturday morning. Tomorrow the Land Rover won't be available to bring us back to Bollobhpur, so we'll have to walk home!

There are children everywhere – laughing, chattering, giggling, all looking surprisingly strong and healthy. They love bathing and running up and down the riverbank. When one takes a photograph they become very straight-faced and afterwards burst into giggles again. There are cows, goats, and chickens everywhere too. Next door to the hospital is an orphanage of eighty-six children and when I went over to visit a few afternoons ago they sang and danced so beautifully that my eyes began to fill up with tears. I was taken on a tour of the orphanage accompanied by crowds of children all hanging onto my hands and clothes.

Benny and I have a newly built bungalow with thick walls and shuttered windows. There is no glass in the windows and it's very cool inside. Both bedrooms have a table and chair. The floors are made of the same sand-and-lime surface as in the main house, buffed and polished. The bathroom is divided into two areas by a low stone wall, on the one side a simple squat toilet and on the other a wide, shallow terracotta tub which is re-filled with water every day by *Joton*, the watercarrier. A bucket serves both to flush the toilet and to throw water over ourselves in order to stay cool and clean. It's now 7.00 p.m. and dark, and a goatherd is walking down the road outside the house playing his pipe as he takes his goats back to the village.

The mission house is a big 'colonial' style bungalow with lofty ceilings. We eat breakfast and lunch on the veranda overlooking the river where ducks and fishermen pass by occasionally. We have supper at 7.30 p.m. in the main room sitting round a large table, then relax till 10.00 p.m. reading and playing scrabble or chess. An old guitar has been found, so hardly an evening goes by without a few songs. Across the garden there's a crumbling gothic-style church – no glass in the windows, of course, and no doors. The bell rings hourly throughout the day and we can hear the villagers singing from the house.

The hospital has thirty-five beds divided into obstetrics, medicine and surgery. At present there are twenty obstetric patients and ten other general beds occupied by patients with a variety of conditions, including chest infections, TB, ulcers, jaundice and surgical cases. There is no running water and electricity is only available when the generator is working.

The *rogies* (patients) are fed by their *shongis* (companions) who are in attendance much of the time. They wander in and out of the ward, cooking food in the compound and often climbing into bed if they feel inclined to have a snooze. Under each bed the *shongis* store sacks of rice, bundles of clothes and anything else that their patient might need. It's hard to keep the chickens and dogs out of the wards, but, when they do appear, they are quickly chased out. Taking everything into consideration, this tiny hospital achieves marvellous results.

Now it's dark in the big house and I'm writing by paraffin lamp again. The generator has not worked since it last broke down!

My New Colleagues
Benny is a tremendous chap. He's a very clever doctor, having graduated with honours eighteen months ago at *Vellore* Medical School in South India. His father is Professor of Preventative Medicine and his mother is a Physiologist at the University Hospital. We will be a good team because his knowledge of general and tropical medicine, together with my experience in paediatrics and obstetrics, will be fundamental. There is no other reliable medical service within sixty miles!

Florence is a remarkable lady in her late fifties who appears to be far more at home out here than when I first met her in Bristol earlier this year. She has built this hospital up from nothing in twenty-five years. She runs the hospital, purchases the equipment and supervises the orphanage where, together with the local priest, she arranges marriages between the orphan girls and local boys. Meg and Pat are nursing sisters who assist in running the hospital and the nursing school and organise the large vaccination and preventive health clinics in the surrounding villages. All three are long-term workers of the Church Missionary Society. Eryl and Lizzie, who are both with Voluntary Services Overseas, assist Florence, Meg and Pat in the busy life of the hospital, nursing patients, delivering babies, teaching the student nurses, giving physiotherapy, dispensing the drugs and anything else that the day may require.

Our nurses come from the local villages and undertake a two-year national certificate course in General Nursing and Midwifery at the hospital. Some continue working at Bollobhpur for many years becoming highly skilled and competent, while others leave to get married or move on in their nursing careers to bigger hospitals.

Lizzie also helps Meg organise our meals, which are really good. It seems I won't go short of food here, although I'm already getting nostalgic for such things as cheese and sausages! The meals are cooked in the kitchen on a simple mud stove. Should an oven be required a metal tin is placed on the top. Everything is produced locally – vegetables from the garden, fish from the river, goat meat from the local herd. There is little milk since the cows produce such small quantities and, even then, it is often watered down before we get it. Bread, butter and jam are always available and, of course, there is the inevitable rice.

27 November

Getting Up to Speed

Well, I'm certainly going to be a wiser man by the time I return! The medical cases here are classic: heart disease, kidney failure, asthma, pneumonia, alongside surgical and orthopaedic patients, premature babies and the very old. They collect outside the hospital in large numbers and we see up to two hundred outpatients in a day, admitting any serious ones who would benefit from the limited treatment that we can offer. The responsibility is both exhilarating and frightening, but when the patients improve and are discharged it gives a real sense of achievement.

For example, last week a four-year-old girl was admitted with what Benny thought may have been tuberculous meningitis. She was completely rigid and deeply unconscious and remained so until yesterday when she opened her eyes and looked around. Today she said a word or two and I can't describe how wonderful it felt.

A few days after the caesarean section, we admitted a patient with a ruptured uterus – an obstetric calamity. She had been in labour for three or four days and had travelled for six hours in a bullock cart before she arrived. Learning that it is not unheard of for village women to go to the extreme measure of standing on a mother's stomach to deliver a baby, we battled for two hours, but could save neither mother or infant. Such patients are often beyond our help, having left the condition too late to come to the hospital.

I'm now waiting to perform another caesarean section on a woman who will almost certainly die if I don't. It is certainly a frightening prospect operating with such limited anaesthetic facilities, a generator which seldom works and no available blood for transfusion. But we can only do our best with God's help. Things are improving, and we have already achieved results that would have been impossible a month ago.

It looks as though I will be operating for much of the time using reflected sunlight! A mirror outside the window reflects the sunlight onto another one suspended above the patient. This gives a bright beam of light exactly where I need it. As the sun moves across the sky the mirrors are adjusted and the table is pushed up the room to catch the shifting light. It sounds impossible, but it works!

I should point out that the 'operating theatre' and the 'delivery suite' are, in fact, the same room, with the surgical table and the delivery table facing in opposite directions, a few feet separating them. There lies the possibility, of course, that the two could be in use at the same time. We can only wait and see!

A prayer is said before a patient is anaesthetised, which has a very calming effect on both the patient and the obstetrician! I'd better stop writing now and go across to the hospital to see if we are ready for the CS.

I'm already learning a lot about humility, content, compassion and kindness from all around me. As Saint Paul puts it: "*Come close to God and he will come close to you.*"

2 December Sunday

Today Lizzie and I walked three and a half miles to *Rotnapur* village to meet Tom and Dianne, a couple from the Church Missionary Society who run an intermediate technology school and the church there. Lizzie was easy to talk to and we had lots to share as we walked along the dusty roads passing rice fields, abandoned old houses, overgrown temples and palm trees. We saw monkeys everywhere. Lizzie is the practical one at the hospital, not only an excellent nurse and midwife, but seems to have a natural gift to mend anything that is broken. Then back for dinner.

I found a tiny lizard running over my bed last night, but over here they're supposed to be lucky.

4 December Tuesday

Learning the Ropes
I've settled in very well. It's a happy place to be working in. Florence, Meg and Pat, Lizzie, Eryl and Benny work extremely hard and are very pleasant to be with. We have *ruti* (unleavened flat bread) for breakfast at 7.15 a.m. and begin ward rounds at 8.00 a.m., which makes it a long day. We have a rice dish for lunch and an 'English' dinner at 7.30 p.m., followed by a quiet evening, reading or playing cards by lamplight. Everyone is glad to get to bed by 10.00 p.m. What with ward rounds in

the morning and evening, huge clinics of up to two hundred patients seen by a couple of us, performing sterilizations one minute, setting fractures or suturing tendons the next, it is a busy life.

Our caesarean lady survives, even though she had a haemoglobin of 20% when we operated. It's quite remarkable that she's still here – a real miracle. The next breath-holding moment comes in two days' time when we take the sutures out. I'm going to have to get used to these emotional ups and downs – elated spirits one minute, followed by anxieties the next. There is so much illness here: rheumatic fever, kidney disease, TB, hypertension, tetanus, peripheral vascular disease – the list goes on and on. One can feel inadequate and sometimes not know what to do for the best. But it's good to have Benny around to share the medical problems. He does baseline tests in his little make-do lab, and they are a major help.

Road Traffic Accident

We managed to get the X-ray machine working for the first time. It arrived last year when aid poured into Bangladesh after the civil war. There are two problems though – firstly, hardly any instructions came with it and secondly, a reliable supply of electricity is essential to make it work! A little girl had been knocked over by a goat and had broken her femur. The X-ray gave us a clear image of the fracture and I manipulated her femur into a good position before we put her into Russell's traction. We couldn't help laughing as we reflected that road accidents happen out here, even though there are only two motor vehicles within a ten-mile radius!

I've seen more disease here in these last two weeks than I have in the previous two years, so as you can imagine there's a steep learning curve ahead. The supply of drugs varies. We can treat a variety of cases one week and then we run out of even aspirin the next. Some of the drugs which arrived with the emergency relief last year are completely inappropriate and we bury them in a large hole in the grounds of the hospital. I hope I'm giving you an idea of the medical situation and expect that I'll be describing more cases in the months to come.

On Sundays at 7.00 a.m. we go to the Bengali services in the village church which is situated about fifty yards from the hospital. German missionaries built it a hundred years ago and it looks the worse for wear. No glass in the windows, of course, and reed mats on the floor, but filled with villagers every week. The collection consists of anything from sacks of rice to chickens which are auctioned outside the door of the church after the service. Last week's Holy Communion, from the Church of North India Prayerbook, followed closely the text of the Book of Common Prayer, but one can scan through the equivalent English prayers at least three times faster than the Bengali!

A Long Walk Home from *Meherpur*

We have a small hospital for *poates* (obstetric patients) and a large general outpatient clinic in *Meherpur*, which, you will remember, is the nearest town. The Land Rover was not available to bring us back so, having seen about two hundred patients in a frantic clinic, we started walking the ten miles back to Bollobhpur along the rutted, dusty roads. It was dark by 5.30 p.m., but we had torches until they began to flicker as the batteries ran out. The miles passed very quickly as we talked and sang, crossing the river on the bamboo ferry, before finally getting back to Bollobhpur three and a half hours later, happy and not tired at all – not even stiff legs!

On Sunday, we walked down the river to Tom and Di's and it was a delight – mango trees, monkeys in the branches, vultures, villagers, fishermen, dogs, and children. Walking three miles there and three miles back is nothing now.

7 December Friday

Nothing That Love Cannot Face

The jackals are howling outside the house. Many thanks for your letter, which I received today, telling me about Princess Anne's wedding last month. It's quiet here now and I'm writing by lamplight, sending you an early Christmas greeting. Last evening we had a log fire for the first time and practised a carol or two. It's getting rather chilly in the evenings and also at breakfast which we eat on the veranda. Each day is filled with a wide variety of medical and surgical patients, many of whom we can treat as successfully here as we do at home, and that gives us great satisfaction. My initial anxiety and concerns about seeing such great numbers of patients and making so many important decisions have gradually diminished. One morning last week I was reading 1 Corinthians 13.1-7 and, as if I were meant to read it, I came across: "*There is nothing love cannot face. There is no limit to its faith, its hope and its endurance.*" I found new strength from that reassurance and now I try to say the verse each morning before I get out of bed. Before all the operations and the difficult and sometimes hurtful decisions that I must now make in this stage of my professional life, I hope I will remember that there is *nothing* that love cannot face.

As the days get cooler, it's perfect for lying out on the lawn after lunch for twenty minutes – very much like a hot June day at home. The lawn slopes down to the river so it's really very pleasant. Already we're thinking about what we'll eat at Christmas! The girls are trying to locate a goose, although I must admit I have a craving for duck at the moment.

16 December

A Difficult Decision and a Trip to the Catholic Fathers
It's been a particularly hot day, although it was very cold at 7.00 a.m. The dogs are barking and the church bell is ringing as I write. We admitted a local politician yesterday with an acute intestinal obstruction. This has a poor prognosis and an operation is imperative. Unfortunately, we have neither sufficient intravenous fluids or the instruments for such major surgery although I would have been willing to undertake it had there been no alternative. We decided that the safest solution would be to drive him a hundred miles north across ferries and along mud roads to the nearest mission hospital at *Radshahi,* where they are better equipped to do such surgery. So, despite a tummy upset in the night, I woke up this morning prepared

for a long drive, not expecting to arrive at the hospital before late afternoon. However, when I went over to the hospital, I discovered that the patient had sadly died during the night.

Later in the morning we got an invitation to the Roman Catholic Mission five miles away for lunch. Meg and Pat being away in Calcutta, I drove the Land Rover across the rough roads to the mission where the local orphan children danced for us and then we feasted on homemade pasta and duck which seemed to have been an answer to prayer! We sat on the veranda looking at the brilliantly coloured flowers, palm trees and ponds in the garden, all bathed in the tropical sunshine.

Many a Slip

It has been quite an eventful week. On Friday evening, Florence and I were invited to Father Tom's at *Rotnapur* for dinner. It now seems quite normal that we should walk the three miles there and we covered the first part of the journey as the sun was setting, walking the last mile by torchlight. *Driver* came over in the Land Rover later to bring us back.

We had an unexpected visit a few days ago from the Director of VSO International, making sure Lizzie and Eryl were alright. He is responsible for over thirteen hundred volunteers worldwide, among whom are teachers, engineers and nurses. He was understandably impressed by what was going on here in this tiny hospital miles from anywhere.

We have a big oval table in the main room where we eat, and dinner that evening was made even more memorable when Lizzie appeared from the other room, slipped on the polished floor and disappeared right underneath the table around which the rest of us were sitting! After ensuring that she was unharmed, there were gales of laughter all round!

A Busy Life

Medically speaking it's been a busy week with worries, triumphs and disappointments all mingled together. The caesarean lady went home looking fine, just fifteen days after I had operated on her believing that she would not survive. One day, I sutured a lady who had been gored by a bull. Another patient I opened up to find widespread cancer. The only thing I could do was close her up again and trust that she would be well enough to go home.

We have had deaths too, many more than you'd expect at home, but there is some comfort in the knowledge that little else could have been done for them in these extreme circumstances. Their poor condition on arrival would have presented huge problems even in the UK with all its medical advantages. We have had several babies with tetanus, a little boy with liver failure, and another little chap with severe anaemia. I would love to have a blood bank here because just a pint of blood may have saved him. Two recent obstetric cases would certainly have survived had blood been available. A blood bank would really make a difference between life and death for many patients and could be set up for as little as £100.

Another baby was very poorly with pneumonia. Thank the Lord, many others respond to treatment and that makes it all so worthwhile.

Plans for a Trip to Calcutta
If things turn out as planned, I will be taking a couple of days off in February to go to Calcutta with Tom and I am sure it will be a welcome break. Benny and I share nights on call, but, living in such a small community, one is very much a part of what's going on twenty-four hours a day and, when there's an emergency 'being off duty' is immediately forgotten. However, it's all very wonderful and I am happy here every moment of every day.

26 December Wednesday

A Cheerful Christmas
Christmas Eve was just like home, everyone hastily wrapping up presents, putting the finishing touches to the decorations, making mince pies and listening to the carols from King's College

Cambridge. Then we joined the villagers for midnight communion in the church. It was really moving, the church filled with villagers and was lit by oil lamps, everyone leaving their shoes outside and sitting cross-legged on prayer mats on the floor. The service was, of course, in *Bangla* (Bengali), but since it runs along the same order as at home and the tunes are familiar, it was easy to follow both the Bengali carols and the Christmas gospel. Then up to the altar rails to receive communion (men from one side of the church, followed by the women from the other) then out into the cold, clear, star-filled night and a "*subhor boro din*" (Happy Christmas) to all and everyone. Finally we all departed, happy and excited and huddled in blankets and shawls.

Christmas morning started at 5.00 a.m. when the nurses and orphans arrived at the bungalow singing carols Bengali style with handclapping and dancing, before they went off to sing around the village, leaving us to get a few more hours of sleep.

The day itself dawned, hot and sunny. It was like a Whitsun treat, everyone crowding around the mission house and packing into the church where the local *Son Kerton* bands of drums, cymbals and bells accompanied the singers, whose songs had been especially composed for the celebration.

And then there were the children, hundreds of them of every age and size, dressed up in their new clothes, swarming around the churchyard, the house, the garden, and in front of the hospital. There was a near riot when we gave out balloons and those little animals you had sent. They besieged the steps of the house and knocked over the marigolds in the rush. You could tell the siblings because they were wearing new dresses and new shirts made from the same material, little girls carrying their baby sisters on their hips. So many beautiful children with their complexions and dark eyes. This is a land of children. And happy too, even though many of them have at least seven or eight siblings with neither a toy or a shoe to share between them. Christmas Day was *their* day as they joined all the other villagers to celebrate the birth of Jesus and their joy and faith was infectious! As we stood on the steps of the house giving presents to the nurses and the orphans, the *Son Kerton* bands crossed over from the church where they had been playing all day, to sing one song after another until it was quite dark and the children were taken home to tea and we retired for half an hour's rest before dinner.

While all these wild celebrations were going on, the hospital had had a particularly busy day with five deliveries, a burns case and the usual number of casualties and calamities. Benny was on duty and dealt with the problems as they arrived.

By the late afternoon both Benny, who had been working throughout the day, and ourselves, who had been contending with the crowds, were exhausted! We enjoyed Christmas dinner at 6.00 p.m. around the big table, which had been decorated with candles, crackers and flowers. Eleven of us sat down to eat, including Rebecca, a seventeen-year-old, who has arrived from Devon, together with a seventy-three-year-old missionary from Calcutta, plus Tom and Dianne from *Rotnapur*. We ate in grand style and, although the brandy failed to light up the 'poor man's' Christmas pudding, we finished with fruit, nuts and homemade toffee and peppermint which Lizzie and Eryl had been busily preparing throughout the previous week.

Then we went into the other room to open a mountain of presents in front of a roaring fire. As you can imagine with eleven of us, there was great fun and laughter as the gifts were opened, which were mostly insignificant things like packets of soup, pins, books, biro refills, ink cartridges, Stero-tabs and shaving soap. When all the presents had been given out, we sang Christmas carols in front of the fire, preferring the more traditional illumination of oil-lamps and candles, though the generator was now working. Then we gathered up the mounds of paper, collected our simple gifts and, after one final verse of *O Come All Ye Faithful*, said goodnight to each other.

Today has seen the annual Boxing Day sports. What great fun! People milling around the little stalls especially erected on the sides of the road and watching every sort of race, including the 'old man's race' in which some of the ancient villagers with weather-beaten faces, white hair, and sinewy limbs, girded up their loincloths and made a sixty-yard sprint down to the finishing line accompanied by shouts of encouragement from everyone. It was an incredibly happy occasion and still the bands and the singing went on. While all this was going on, I had been working my way through the men's clinic, but thank heavens, only forty or so of them turned up!

Many thanks for your wonderful Christmas parcel which gave us all so much pleasure as we opened the different compartments. The decorations were used to decorate the nurses' chapel with its open sides, thatched roof and polished floor. The children from the orphanage absolutely loved the card games and rapidly learned how to play Snap, shouting at the top of their voices. There was near bedlam when I gave out the animals to the village children. I'm sure they will be valued, as they were possibly the first toys that they'd ever had. The writing paper will be extremely useful over the next few months and the *Sunday Express* has already been read from cover to cover by everyone in turn. We all send our grateful thanks – *Onek Donabard* (Thank you).

We are now sitting on the lawn behind the house looking over the river, with the parrots screeching and the bees buzzing. At last, we have time to reflect on the Christmas celebration. I will especially remember the hundreds of children, laughing and happy in their new dresses and shirts, the flowers and the sunshine, the local bands playing Bengali carols, a goose for Christmas dinner, the 'poor man's' Christmas pudding, homemade crackers and all the treasured customs of East and West combined into one.

Chapter 2

1974

5 January

Learning the Language

I'm trying to learn one new Bengali phrase every day! Repeating it many times in a morning's clinic helps to build up my language skills. But the phrases sometimes get muddled. I couldn't understand why some patients were hyperventilating when I was asking them to open their mouth (*"Aah koro"*) until it was pointed out that I was saying *"Nishash Naam"* which means *"breathe in and out"*! On other occasions, I've asked patients to lie on the table and they've promptly got up and walked out of the room. I was gently told by one of the nurses that I was telling them to *"go round to the pharmacy window"*!

As you can imagine our pharmacy is frantic on clinic days. Medicines, like cough mixtures and antacids, solutions of gentian violet and lotions to treat scabies are dispensed in bottles brought by the patients. The drugs in pill form are dispensed in little cones made out of old newspapers. Of course they often arrive from the relief organisations in small white boxes and the village children frequently ask for a box so that they can put a stone in it to make a rattle.

All our nurses have lovely Bengali names: *Mena, Onapona, Kolpona, Rochena, Malotti, Bedona, Niha, Monju, Tunu and Togor.* Such is the instinctive nature of their belief (and everyone else's) that despite the deprivations they cannot understand why so many people in England don't believe in God.

After a hectic week, things look a little more settled and I'm keeping my fingers crossed that the situation would remain so. We've had the generator working since Christmas, so we have lighting in both the hospital and the big house after dark which makes everything a little easier. Unfortunately the electricity doesn't get as far as the bungalow, so we still go to bed in a little pool of lamplight which is very relaxing. We don't have running water and I shave in cold pump water.

Our clinics have been particularly heavy lately and we've admitted a lot of ill people, including two patients with eclampsia (life-threatening seizures in pregnant women). Although considered to be a calamity at home we heavily sedated them and they are still with us and improving daily. Thank heavens for so many miracles!

Each day I learn new skills and techniques – amputating fingers, assessing burns, treating cardiac failure whilst at the same time, praying that someone's peptic ulcer doesn't perforate. It's been remarkably busy, but I hope we'll have a quiet day before the next emergency. Marvellous really!

The drug situation is good and we can treat most things. But then we run out of such basic things as aspirin for a while and it becomes more difficult.

Benny has gone to a dental conference to learn better techniques for extracting teeth. I am slowly improving my dentistry skills too – how these manuals come in useful! The villagers must endure dreadful toothache before they come to the hospital for a painful tooth to be removed.

Without access to toothbrushes the villagers use the frayed ends of twigs, piled with ash, to clean their teeth. This seems to be efficient in younger people whose teeth are always attractive, but the practice doesn't appear to have long-lasting benefits since we see so much gum disease in older patients.

Oral hygiene is made somewhat worse because of the habitual chewing of *paan* (betel nut) by the villagers for its mild stimulant effect. Unfortunately, the saliva becomes red and is spat out quite randomly, so not only do you see teeth and gums stained red, but also stains up the wall wherever you look!

I'm recovering from a temperature of 104 and still feel very weak. Lizzie brought me a plate of scrambled egg – the most amazing scrambled egg I have ever tasted. She *is* a good cook!

10 January

A Wedding in the Village

On New Year's Day, we were invited to a wedding feast in the village. In this tiny place, in the middle of nowhere, we sat on the ground together with a hundred and fifty others. No-one is ever turned away from a wedding, so all the local children and beggars came too and were all treated with the same hospitality. After prayers, the feast began with rice and curry coming round by the bucketful and served on banana leaves in front of us, until we couldn't eat any more and our lips were burning. The celebration went on until dark, when oil lamps began to appear and the dogs began to bark. Then, after grateful *"Onek donabards"* all round we walked back through the darkened village to the hospital, knowing that another hundred and fifty people would sit down soon after, the wedding couple sitting solemnly on the veranda of the family house throughout the whole proceedings.

13 January

A Welcome Break

Please excuse the oil stain from the hurricane lamp which has mysteriously dribbled onto the writing paper! I've just come back after twenty-four hours at Tom and Dianne's in *Rotnapur,* three miles away. It was my first night away from the hospital in eight weeks and I was extremely glad of the break. Lizzie and Eryl walked halfway with me in the hot afternoon sunshine. We wandered alongside the river, passing solitary fishermen and villagers bathing. Then through yellow fields of mustard, linseed, mango groves and paddy fields and along the furrowed road to *Rotnapur* passing goats, oxcarts, and men carrying loads of hay and jute on their heads. At every stage of the journey, we were accompanied by happy children.

What a lovely weekend away from it all, listening to Beethoven on the gramophone, playing cards and reading. Most of the time I just sat, grateful for a few hours' peace. Thank you for sending that book about the Festival of Light which I enjoyed very much and read from cover to cover in an afternoon.

Every Obstetrician's Nightmare

I had a stressful time in the operating theatre last Thursday evening. I was performing a caesarean section on a woman who had been in obstructed labour for several days. I delivered a chubby eight-pound baby who proceeded to scream the place down. Then disaster happened – I couldn't stop the bleeding. We have no diathermy here and the more arteries I tied off, the more she bled. No doubt the reasons for this haemorrhaging included her long labour, her poor condition and my own inexperience. Her blood pressure was dropping and after two hours we were all sick with worry. I could feel my strength and concentration draining away. So many prayers went up, "*Please God, let me get her off the table alive.*" We were really beginning to despair. Then suddenly the bleeding points *did* stop. I don't know how – I didn't think I'd stopped them. I sewed up quickly, drenched in perspiration. Everyone was thankful. The patient was transferred back into her bed alive, yet in an extremely poor condition. Miracles seem to be happening every day here. It must be the result of everyone's prayers at home, I know, because so many people pray for us. We cleaned up, had a cup of tea, and sat around and said a prayer, "*...defend us from all perils and dangers of this night.*" I slept in the little room above the operating theatre and got up to see her at 3.00 a.m. and 5.00 a.m. Just as night was over and the sun was rising on a cold clear Friday, the poor mother died. But that's just an example of many such days and nights in this extraordinarily fulfilling life. I'm much rested now and ready to tackle the new week, God willing.

18 January Friday

A Painful Abscess

Another caesarean section in the early hours of Monday morning! Thankfully, all went to plan and the mother is doing surprisingly well. I developed an abscess ten days ago, which was becoming increasingly painful. Florence incised it yesterday. Ouch! Now I'm all trussed up like a chicken but quite relieved of pain and well enough to carry out ordinary work. I've already done three sterilizations this morning.

Tomorrow I'm having a few days off to properly recover and I'm looking forward to it. Florence and I are driving down to *Khulna*. We're taking two Land Rovers full of the children who are going back to their school at *Barisal*, the institution referred to around here as 'Douglas Boarding'. Exactly who Douglas was, I have yet to find out! The school was founded by the Oxford Mission Fathers. Alongside the school, I understand, there is a maternity hospital, where its lone doctor (one of the sisters of the community) sees a vast number of women every week. Many people would prefer to go to mission hospitals for treatment rather than the government institutions because they get treated so badly there.

The trip should be fun. We'll probably stay at the 'Save the Children' hostel and even manage a Chinese meal somewhere! I won't have travelled so far away from the village since I arrived.

Our senior nurse, *Tunu*, has left Boll. to get married next year. She has been working here for twenty years and is much respected for her knowledge and experience. Her departure has caused great sadness and many tears, but we are all looking forward to her wedding in the Spring.

20 January Sunday

The Football Results and a Picnic on the Banks of the Ganges

It's getting dark now and I can hear the generator starting up across at the hospital a hundred yards away. This afternoon we listened to the Sunday Service on the crackling BBC World Service followed by the news and the football results. Each week there is great excitement as our home teams get mentioned! Today Newport County drew their match at home. Amazing to get such up-to-date local sports news here in this little village on the far side of the globe!

Earlier in the week Benny, Lizzie, Eryl, Rebecca and I had to go to *Kushtia* to register our presence in Bangladesh. The town is about a two-hour drive north of Bollobhpur. On the way we had a picnic on the banks of the Ganges. As usual, our presence offered an immediate attraction to all the children and adults in the district and, within twenty minutes of sitting down on the grass, we had sixty spectators standing around us in a silent circle, watching us eat. We had great fun. After the lengthy process of registering, we spent some time shopping for bread and drugs before driving back along the bumpy roads. Driving anywhere in Bangladesh is very tiring, even if you're sitting in the back of a Land Rover.

27 January Sunday

News of the Political Crisis at Home

Greetings from Bollobhpur on another sunny Sunday morning! I hope you notice I'm using the writing paper left over from my twelve hours' stay in that Bangkok hotel on the journey out last October. You'll remember that we had landed in the middle of a *coup d'état* which confined us to the building. You can imagine how expensive paper is over here when I tell you that even toilet rolls cost the equivalent of fourteen shillings – far beyond our means! Still, we are well compensated for the absence of such luxuries by the fact that tomatoes can be bought for tuppence a pound!

I've got a day off today, so I'm beginning another round of letter writing, answering the many people who send me letters. We're all thrilled when the post comes on a Monday or a Thursday, about ten days after you post them. We had a dear old missionary lady staying with us over Christmas who said that in the old days letters took about three months to arrive from England.

I do hope that the political situation at home isn't becoming too much of a worry. If there were to be an election soon (which I notice that some of the papers are already predicting), I would give my support to Ted Heath, for heaven knows what will happen if anyone else gets in. We keep up to date with news by reading the *Weekly Guardian*, which is sent out to Lizzie and Eryl, but keenly read by all of us in turn. It's great for keeping in touch with what's going on at home but takes nearly the whole week to plough through. Pat spends much time trying to complete the crossword before the next edition arrives and Benny attacks the chess problem even before the paper is out of its cover!

I read that house prices at home have gone up by 115% since 1970 and petrol prices have risen by 43% this year! Our shared view is that austerity will bring everyone back to a simpler way of living, which is what we enjoy here. We find pleasure in simple things such as sitting around the fire in the evening reading, playing chess or listening to music. To be thrilled at the sight of a bowl of soup or a very occasional piece of cheese; to lie under a blue sky listening to the birds and watching the fishermen – each moment brings its own happiness. At present I am earning ten shillings a month – who could want anything more!

3 February

Another Sunday afternoon with parrots squawking all around the house and the wards quiet for a little while. It's another glorious day, but the winter is over and it's starting to get just a little too hot to stay out on the lawn for long. We were invited out to lunch today in the village, so once again we were sitting on the veranda of a family home (no tables or chairs, of course) demolishing great mounds of rice, delicious goat meat and vegetables, with the spices stinging our lips and fingers. We were most grateful! The hosts always stand and watch their guests eat, eating only after their visitors have departed. It was an especially good meal because we had been invited to a wedding feast a couple of weeks ago but, when the time came for us to join the wedding party, they had forgotten to call us – quite a blunder in village etiquette, I am told.

Tomorrow I'm off for a week's holiday with Tom, so next week I hope to be writing to you from Calcutta. This will make a pleasant change. There's a great deal of shopping for food, drugs and equipment to be done, but I hope there will also be time for some sightseeing. The prospect of travelling to the big city is exciting.

13 February

A Week in Calcutta

Last week Tom and I went down to *Jessore* where there is a border crossing into India. As soon as we crossed over we were struck by the contrast: market stalls laden with food, fruit and household goods, which are so scarce in rural Bangladesh. We also noticed the number of women walking freely in the streets, dressed in colourful saris. One seldom sees women in a Muslim country like Bangladesh and you can go for miles without ever seeing one, although the Christian villages are different. India seems all bustle and life after four months in the countryside.

We travelled on a crowded train about sixty miles south to Calcutta, arriving at 10.30 p.m. What a city! Huge, sprawling, absolutely filthy, broken pavements, heaps of dirt piled up on them, decaying houses and buildings, shacks and shops, people living and sleeping on the streets and in the stations, beggars everywhere, some without arms or legs, others deformed or blind, all wearing tattered clothes, the rickshaws pulled by emaciated men. Depressing, yes, because of its dismal poverty and overcrowding, but nonetheless vibrant, for everyone is busy doing something or selling something, if only to stay alive.

There are some modern streets too, in the middle of all the dilapidated buildings, where we found bookshops, restaurants and markets selling everything from exotic fruits and flowers to clothes and medical equipment. Having been out in the remote villages for so long, it was just marvellous to be among people again.

Forgotten Cemetery

One day we visited the old British Cemetery which was used between 1780 and 1830. It was at the end of a quiet street, forgotten and neglected, overrun with trees, and creepers climbing up the monuments and graves. Numerous headstones had all but disappeared and the paths were obscured. There was not a soul in sight. The inscriptions on some of the gravestones were heartbreaking: "*Mary*

Bedford aged twenty-two, died 1790"; *"John Price aged twenty-five, died 1824"*; alongside the bigger monuments were little headstones recording the death of infants. So many young men and women must have come out here during those colonial days only to die of tropical disease. It was a most moving experience to see proud forgotten memorials of an empire which had disappeared long ago.

Arrested for Smuggling

After a few days' retreat with the Oxford Mission Fathers at *Behala* in the south of the city, we set off from crowded Sealda Railway Station at about 8.30 a.m., arriving at the border by lunchtime. Then trouble began. Asked to open the cold butter bag which we had crammed full of tetanus vaccines, the customs officials weren't happy and, despite our repeated explanations, we got the distinct feeling that we were being arrested. We were politely asked to remain in a side room for several hours until we were finally given permission to cross back into Bangladesh.

What a relief to see *Driver* and the Land Rover waiting for us on the other side. Another sixty miles north back to Bollobhpur and we arrived at 8.00 p.m. Everybody came out to greet us and catch up with the news of our adventures. I was looking forward to a good wash because the polluted air of Calcutta seems even to penetrate one's skin.

It's been a quieter week since I returned, thank heavens. With the temperature rising to 98 and 99 most afternoons the clinics have been smaller. I'm glad to say that my Bengali is rapidly improving, and as a result the clinics are taking a little less time. There haven't been any obstetric emergencies in the last few days so there has been less to worry about.

19 February Tuesday

The days are getting warmer, and it was just too hot to sit outside in the sun today. But everyone says, *"just you wait for the real hot weather!"* Please don't be worried if you hear news of storms and typhoons. Bollobhpur is so far inland that we only get the tail end of them. The weekend in December that you mentioned in your letter was indeed extremely wet, windy and cold, but we just sat around the fire a little longer than usual and wished that there were more panes of glass in the windows of the house.

26 February

An Approaching Marriage

Earlier this week we attended a preliminary ceremony leading up to the wedding of one of the orphan girls. The bridegroom's father brought three silver bracelets and a variety of gifts, such as a comb, sweets and paint for her hands and feet and a traditional sago-type pudding. After a great deal of singing by the other orphans, the shy little bride, dressed in a new sari, sat on a mat and was fed the pudding by everyone else. Practically speaking, this meant cramming the sago into her mouth till she was nearly bursting, much to the hilarity of everyone! The following day she was covered in yellow powder to make her look fair, and there she sat 'in state' all day while everyone fed her with sweets. It certainly looked a more complicated business than the preparations for an English wedding, and more colourful too!

It would seem another miracle occurred a few days ago when, without any of the essential laboratory tests that we would rely on at home, a comatose diabetic regained consciousness. It was an all-night vigil. Now he is much improved and looking forward to going home. The following night an obstetric problem kept me up all night. The poor lady is progressing well after a very rough twelve hours. I had a good night's sleep last night and I'm feeling fine again now.

Yesterday we travelled to *Meherpur* to bring back a *poate* in a poor state. The return journey was terribly slow because of the state of the road, but the lady delivered a healthy baby on our return to the hospital and is recovering satisfactorily today. However, soon after we had got back to Bollobhpur, another patient in obstructed labour was admitted. She too needed a forceps delivery and, by the time the baby had arrived, the afternoon was gone.

A Tragic Accident

Saturday was a sad day for everyone. Our cheerful cook, *Mogul*, has brought up four boys by herself since her husband died in the refugee camps two years ago. The eldest boy, aged twelve, has been extremely difficult to manage, causing his mother much heartache. On Friday he and his friends climbed onto the church roof and he fell thirty feet to the ground. He sustained a head injury and despite our efforts to save him, he died the following morning. *Mogul* is distraught because, she says, "*I used to hit him so hard.*" Out here in this isolated place we see victories and defeats, triumphs and tragedies, one after another.

6.30 p.m.: They have just told me that a bullock cart is rolling into the hospital compound which doesn't sound so good! I'd better go and investigate...

6.50 p.m.: The mother delivered a baby boy outside the gate, so all is well.

3 March Sunday 5.00 p.m.

I hope that you've received the roll of film that I sent. You'll probably be surprised at the number of photographs of children I've taken, but the kids are everywhere and they can't resist standing in front of a camera! The adults don't photograph well because they line up and become very serious. By the way, don't be surprised if I look a little slimmer on the photos. I've lost a stone already, presently weighing in at 12st 7lb. I haven't been this slender for years. The weight loss is probably due to a combination of hard work, hot weather and a low-fat diet.

I don't know when you'll actually be reading this because the nationwide postal strike is moving into its third week with no sign of abating. Of course, that means that we haven't received any post either, but I hope and pray that everyone is well at home and not too confused by what we understand is an escalating political crisis at home. Hopefully, Meg is flying home on Wednesday, but she hasn't managed to get official permission to leave the country yet. Such things take a long time to sort out over here.

The Water-carrier's Baby

It's been quite an exciting week from a medical point of view. *Joton* is one of the hospital staff. He carries water from the pump to the large water pots in our rooms, the kitchen and the hospital, and does odd jobs around the place. The future of his marriage depended on a live male child but, thankfully, after some anxious hours for all of us, his wife delivered the required baby boy.

On our arrival at *Meherpur* on Wednesday, we found a lady needing an emergency caesarean section and brought her back with us, operating shortly after we had returned. The following day I was doing another caesarean section on a local girl in obstructed labour. Both babies were delivered alive and kicking and we were all delighted. A missionary doctor from Rajshahi Hospital, called Liz, was here in Bollobhpur for a week's holiday and was glad to help me with the second caesar, firstly giving the anaesthetic and then assisting me. She was a real help and very pleasant company.

After the second caesarean section, we had a quick lunch and I drove her down to Chuadanga Station to catch the train back to *Rajshahi*. She was ten minutes late arriving at the station, but the train arrived even later, so all was well.

When we arrived back at Boll. at 6.00 p.m., we found yet another surgical problem, so this morning I was operating again. There weren't any complications and we'd finished by lunchtime. The temperature has now gone up to ninety-six in the afternoons, but I've had a good sleep and woke up for tea feeling grand!

What a surprise election result in February! We were glued to the crackling radio all Friday and since we were six hours in front of you, we heard the first results around breakfast time and from then on the results became increasingly exciting throughout the day. It was a busy clinic that morning and after lunch I amputated a toe. I'd better draw the letter to a close now as my oil lamp is beginning to pop which means dirt in the kerosene and it's a bit difficult to see what I'm writing.

12 March

When to Say Grace

Bishop James Blair has been staying with us over these last few days, whilst confirming children in the surrounding villages. He is an Oxford Mission Father who was consecrated as the first Bishop of Bangladesh. He is an elderly gentleman with a straight back and a broad smile, putting us all at ease at dinner: "*We only say grace with gravy,*" he said.

Benny is off to *Barisal* for a week's holiday tomorrow, so I hope that the hospital remains as quiet as it is at present. We went to a wedding feast yesterday in a nearby village and had a pleasant meal, tons of rice and goat curry. Tomatoes are still in abundance, huge and juicy; we have them for breakfast, lunch and dinner. But soon the season will be over and we won't see another one until this time next year.

24 March

A Rare Taste of Pork

We had a pleasant change from goat meat this week, when a herd of black pigs appeared in the district. I understand that pig farming has been going on in Bangladesh for as long as anybody can remember and they are reared in roaming herds. The swineherds, who are mostly low caste Hindus, take them from location to location every year, grazing for food and selling one or two pigs in non-Muslim villages as they move northwards. After a six-month abstinence, the smell and taste of roast pork was divine, although I must admit the meat was a bit tough!

A Busy Week

Benny came back from *Barisal* today and although it hasn't been a desperately busy week it was good to see him back. When I say "*it hasn't been a desperately busy week*" I should say that I saw about a hundred and fifty people at the Meherpur hospital, followed by a ward round and a check of all the babies there, before coming back to Bollobhpur. Then I was up in the night doing a forceps delivery. By the time I got back to bed, the dawn was coming up. I got up early for the men's clinic and saw another hundred and twenty patients. So it wasn't a particularly busy week! Thankfully, there were no emergencies. But, yes, it *was* good to see Benny back!

The seasons are changing again. It is noticeably hot and sticky early in the mornings and the air is becoming progressively heavier throughout the day. I'm told that from now on it will get increasingly humid until the rains come in June. Benny slept outside on the veranda last night, but I won't join him for a while yet. As it gets warmer, we are getting strong winds in the evenings, blowing all the trees and banging all the shutters. It's quite exhilarating, but I understand that they will only last for a few weeks and then it will be back to the stillness and the heat.

Beautiful Skies

What incredible skies we are seeing now! Yesterday at sunset, the colours were breathtaking! Indigos and blues and all shades of greens, reds, pinks and oranges, with dark purple clouds lined with gold. *"The heavens are telling the glory of God!"*

Today I was lying on my back simply overawed as I watched the colours constantly changing above me. I was thinking of those colour cards that are used at home, when one wants to choose a new paint for the bathroom.

A Case for Family Planning

Two Canadian doctors, Malika and Patsy, have been staying with us and giving talks to the nurses and local women about family planning, which is taking such a long time to catch on in Bangladesh. Considering how fast the population is growing, the consequences are frightening. At the present time, girls get married at fourteen or fifteen and then go on to produce children until either they die in childbirth or are just too old to bear anymore. Many of the obstetric emergencies that I see involve women who already have thirteen or fourteen children. Unless the Bengalis start limiting their families soon, one cannot see any hope of progress. The Christian villages are accepting this responsibility well, and here in the hospital I'm doing about four or five sterilizations a week.

Here's a lovely prayer I found:

O Lord our God, you are in every place. We thank you that no space or distance can separate us from you, and that those who are absent from each other are still present with you. Have in your holy keeping those from whom we are now separated, and grant that both they, and we, by drawing near to you, may be drawn nearer to each other.

Through Jesus Christ our Lord.

4 April Thursday 5.00 p.m.

It's extremely hot and sultry this afternoon. I'm sitting in my swimming trunks in the house with a garland of flowers around my neck which the village children have just made for me. I'm listening to the distant thunder, and I think the rain is going to pour down very soon. You can hear a storm approaching like a steam train coming towards you. We begin the clinics earlier and earlier these days. This morning I did a D&C at 7.45 a.m. followed by a quick ward round and began the men's clinic at 8.15 a.m. I saw a hundred and thirty-six patients by lunchtime at 1.45 p.m. Today we had a goat curry. Goat meat is gorgeous and there is always loads of rice, lentils, bananas and tomatoes. This afternoon I incised a few abscesses and then had an opportunity to read your letter. The rain is absolutely lashing down now, but it's nice and dry in the house and cool for the first time today.

9 April

Palm Crosses

Last Sunday was Palm Sunday. The children of the village were up early making palm crosses and, by the middle of the morning, there were simply hundreds of them. The church was crowded, everybody holding up crosses and waving palm branches. Then, as we sang the Bengali equivalent of *All Glory, Laud and Honour*, we processed around the outside of the church. The children had great fun, their crosses now dry, having earlier been green and moist with dew.

Florence is flying to Nepal tomorrow for a missionary conference and she is looking forward to a rest. Dianne (Tom's wife) is expecting her first baby sometime soon and we are hoping that everything will be alright. It's a bit worrying because we're so inaccessible out here, but her pregnancy has gone well so far.

We've been having tremendous thunderstorms lately. At noon yesterday it was completely overcast before the rain lashed down for hours. My consulting room got so dark that I could hardly see my antenatal patients. Soon the whole of the compound turned into mud and there were pools of water everywhere as the rain poured off the roofs, but by the evening it was lovely again with another incredible sky and the air was fresh and cool.

Pat and Becky came back from Calcutta and we all enjoyed catching up with their news. Becky has bought me a book on Toulouse-Lautrec and I'm looking forward to reading it. At the moment I'm in the middle of another fascinating book about Nicholas and Alexandra and the Russian Revolution. It's been a quiet week without any really worrying cases and we've had plenty of time to read, especially in the early afternoon when it's too hot to work. We get up early in the morning when it's cool and incredibly beautiful and get through the large crowds by lunchtime. The clinics are interspersed with surgery, setting fractures and extracting painful teeth.

A woman was admitted this morning, having been hit over the head by an angry brother-in-law. She needed several sutures and has probably sustained a fractured skull, but the generator hasn't been working for five weeks so we haven't been able to take X-rays to confirm the diagnosis. The only way we can treat head injuries in this remote place is to monitor them. The patient's condition is deteriorating this afternoon and we are praying that she will recover because, if she dies, there will be a lot of trouble with the police.

My most recent caesarean section lady left hospital yesterday, fit and well, with a big chubby baby. There are no operations lined up for tomorrow, so we can look forward to another quiet day.

Removing Cataracts

I may be going north in the summer to one of the government Eye Camps where they sometimes perform a hundred and twenty cataract operations in twenty-four hours. I hope they will teach me how to do this specific eye surgery. Maybe, in the cooler weather, we will be able to have an Eye Camp here for those people with cataracts in the villages around Bollobhpur. The operation itself is not technically difficult, and I will be thrilled if I can help some of the blind people in this area.

I write so many letters and try to stay connected with friends scattered all over the place. I'm afraid my missives might get a little boring, but I hope you enjoy them.

14 April Easter Sunday

A Long Journey for a Little Boy

Easter greetings to you from Bollobhpur! Isn't it wonderful to hear the Resurrection story once again and to know that there is nothing in heaven and earth that can separate us from God's love!

Easter started on Thursday when we admitted a nine-year-old boy with an intestinal obstruction. He was extremely unwell and would probably have died unless he underwent surgery. We debated as to whether I should operate here in Bollobhpur with my limited experience of bowel surgery or whether we should take him the hundred miles north to Rajshahi Mission Hospital, uncertain as to whether he would survive the five-and-a-half-hour journey.

At 8.00 a.m. on Good Friday morning, I decided that he was well enough to travel, so by 8.30 a.m. we were on our way with the little boy in the back of the Land Rover, his drip hanging from the roof. We had a good journey north, crossing rivers on bamboo ferries and over dubious bridges, arriving at the hospital at 2.30 p.m.

After examining him, Dr Malika and I decided to let the little boy rest after the long journey and operate the following day. Early the next morning we found that his condition had improved, his obstruction having partially resolved overnight and the planned operation was probably no longer necessary. A real answer to prayer! Perhaps the very rough journey had been to his advantage. We shall never know, but I did thank God for helping me to make the right decision. What a happy Easter! I was delighted to speak enough *Bangla* to tell the little chap not to worry because the operation was not necessary and that we would now go back to Bollobhpur. I left him there much improved and quite happy. We had a good journey back down south and arrived in time for tea.

Easter Day
Easter morning started early in Bollobhpur. At 4.30 a.m. groups of singers with drums and cymbals began their processions around the villages. They passed by the mission house three times before dawn. Then, at sunrise, all the villagers went down to the cemetery, where the graves had been tidied up and scrubbed. The families stood around each grave with candles and flowers and we sang Easter hymns. The church was full of happy and excited villagers for the communion service at 7.00 a.m. After the service we had a boiled egg for breakfast (a great treat) followed by a quiet ward round, made even more straightforward today because there were no chickens to chase out.

Now it's 12.15 p.m. and Benny and I are just going over for lunch. Florence is still in Nepal. In a day or two, Lizzie, Eryl and Becky are off for five weeks' holiday in *Kashmir* and are looking forward to their break. The birds are singing outside the house and all is peaceful. May your days be full of sunshine.

21 April Sunday

The temperature is now over 102! One is permanently soaking wet with perspiration, but I survive the uncomfortable conditions by sitting here in my swimming trunks and looking forward to a nice cool bucket of water after tea. Poor Lizzie, who was all ready to go to *Kashmir* last Tuesday, came down with a fever of 104 on Monday afternoon. She's still recovering from flu-like symptoms but hopes to travel tomorrow and join Eryl and Rebecca in Delhi.

There was great excitement last week when Benny, who sleeps outside on the veranda, woke up to find two young men searching under his pillows for the keys. He gave me a shout, but I took so much time disentangling myself from the mosquito net that we couldn't catch them. I'm afraid my pens have gone as have our locks. Sadly a lot of stealing goes on here involving the house-staff, the children and sometimes even the patients. One *shongi* was found hiding hospital blankets underneath the body of her recently deceased mother as the bullock cart was going out of the gate. We should learn to give them less opportunity to steal, I suppose.

28 April Sunday

A New Baby
Today has been a memorable day in Bollobhpur. Tom and Di's baby was born at 9.00 a.m. on this cool Sunday morning, with the nurses singing hymns just outside the labour room and a sparrow fluttering round inside; a seven-and-a-half-pound baby girl! She seemed so fair compared with all the darker Bengali babies that we see. Everyone just gazed in wonder.

Dianne was wonderful, behaving in true Bengali fashion, with a rapid labour of only six hours from beginning to end and not requiring even an aspirin for the pains. The responsibility of delivering a colleague's baby out here in the remote countryside of rural Bangladesh has been a heavy one, so it was a great relief all round when the baby arrived safely.

Earlier this evening Tom brought down some of his homemade beer for a little celebration. He said that the brew had become so strong that we would have to dilute it with twice its volume of water, but I think he was pulling our legs. The baby will be called *Susila*.

5 May Sunday

Government Approval

Another Sunday morning already! I'm sitting here in my *lungi* to catch the breeze. A *lungi* is an ankle-length piece of cloth wrapped around the waist. It's already very humid, even before we've gone over to breakfast. Last evening there was a great thunderstorm for several hours with a spectacular display of lightning beforehand. As the clouds rolled in, there was the weirdest light and then it began to rain. And did it rain!

We have so much to be thankful for this week: Dianne's little girl was safely delivered and, even after this short time, she seems to be changing every day. It's quite a novelty having a new baby in the house.

A fifteen-year-old married girl was admitted with TB meningitis earlier in the week. She had completely lost the sight of both eyes. We started treatment and today she said that she could now distinguish people with her left eye as they moved around her. Praise the Lord!

On Friday I did two sterilizations followed by a tricky two-hour operation to amputate an old chap's foot. The whole op. went smoothly. We took the drain out today and it's healing well.

Apparently, our sterilization figures have been received favourably in government departments in *Dhaka*. We seem to be doing as much of this work as anyone else in the country. We were visited by the civil surgeon of the district who promised us pethidine, morphia and other drugs, just as we were getting dangerously low. Population control is the only hope of avoiding a disaster in the near future – the figures are frightening.

One of our nurses *Sumitra*, who took an overdose of pheno-barbitone a fortnight ago and was unconscious for several days, has come back from a week's holiday with all her problems solved. She is back on duty this morning, happy and smiling.

I did a difficult forceps delivery on Tuesday afternoon, resuscitating the baby in between the second and third stages. Just as we were sorting things out, another lady was admitted who was bleeding heavily. But all was well, and everything went satisfactorily.

Lizzie, Eryl and Becky are still in *Kashmir*. I hope to have a week off in June to see my old college friend, Jack Praeger, who runs a clinic in *Saidpur*. While I'm there, I will try to see the Italian Fathers who became such good friends at language school in *Barisal* where I used to give them extra English lessons. They too are up north near *Saidpur*, I believe.

14 May Tuesday

Amputating a Leg

We've had an exciting day today. I'm sitting on the back veranda just before dinner at 7.30 p.m., listening to the distant roll of thunder. There are occasional flashes of lightning, but not much rain yet. I had a good sleep this afternoon. Having removed a big ovarian cyst yesterday and amputated a leg this morning, I was very weary.

The trouble is that when the operation is over you suddenly discover that you're absolutely soaked with sweat and a complete change of clothes is necessary. But *both* patients are doing well and so is the doctor! You will remember the woman with the head injury that I mentioned in a previous letter, sadly she died and the brother-in-law was subsequently arrested for murder. But thank goodness, we've had no trouble from the police. The hospital is quiet tonight. There are no immediate problems or impending crises so, as I say to the patients a hundred times a day, "*Boi nay, ballo hoi jabe*" (Don't worry, it'll soon get better.)

Thank the Lord, the young girl who could not see has progressed well. It's wonderful that now she has only loss of vision in one eye.

25 May

A Need for Blood

Today, I've been told by my colleagues to take a few hours off so I'm writing an early reply. I'm suffering from a bit of a chest infection and sinusitis that has come at the tail end of a cold that's been hanging around for a week or two. I'm sure this day off will help. Yesterday, we drove to *Kushtia* for further registration. It was absolutely roasting and we had to hang about for ages. I was glad to get back to Bollobhpur for a glass of ice-cold water. Anyway, it seems that I'm legally registered in the country at last. It was worth all the heat and dust. I'm very much enjoying writing with this pen. It's new and I bought it for 1/6d. Both my pens, the one given to me by the choir and the other by Latimer Jones, have been pinched, in addition to my suitcase! Things get stolen over here quite frequently.

How good it would be to have a blood bank. A young mother of eighteen died a fortnight ago, simply because we didn't have a pint of blood to give her.

I performed another caesarean section early last Saturday morning and both mother and baby are alive and well. The stitches come out tomorrow. There is a little lull in the work at present and the hospital looks empty, but not for long I expect. That old gentlemen's amputation has healed well. I must think about amputating his other leg, but I am most reluctant to do it as it will leave him so incapacitated. But he is in terrible pain and there just isn't any blood getting through to his leg and foot. I'll be thinking about it more over the next few days.

I'm really looking forward to my second year. Language-wise, I find myself able to speak and understand more Bengali every day. I'm not finding the decision making quite so overwhelming either. We have already dealt with practically every major obstetric disaster in the book, so it's not as stressful any longer.

It is often said in this country, "*May you never be tired!*".

27 May

Rainbows in the Snow
The girls came back from *Kashmir* on Sunday with tales of an amazing time. They had flown to *Srinaga* where they had stayed on a houseboat and eaten great quantities of walnuts and cherries. A

few days later they had taken a bus into the hills as far as *Pahalgam*, a town located at the base of the *Kolahoi* Peak. On their journey northwards they passed lush green fields and fast-flowing streams and had seen a rainbow visible against a background of glistening snow. From *Pahalgam* they trekked ever upwards, well above the snowline, until they had to stop every few steps to catch their breath. They saw spring flowers emerging from the melting snow and had met nomads, whose women wore heavy jewellery and rode on yaks, holding tightly to chickens under their arms!

Having returned south and spent the night in Old Delhi station with the beggars, they endured a two-and-a-half-day journey across North India on a crowded train, standing in that little area at the end of the carriage, so crammed that there was no space to sit down. People were being pushed in and out of the window every time the train stopped for food and water – something of a nightmare, I think, after the splendour of the Himalayas! They were glad to see *Driver* waiting for them on this side of the border.

Counting the Stars

We are spending the evening sitting on the front steps looking at the millions of stars above us. It is quite awesome. The Milky Way is clearly defined, as are the constellations, and we often see shooting stars and satellites as they pass overhead.

The *Son Kerton* bands have been going round the village day after day, praying for the all-important rain. Unless it comes in a few days, the rice harvest will be ruined. It is sad to think that the monsoon is expected to commence in two weeks and it will rain solidly for three months. But then it will be too late.

We get remarkably few post-operative infections here, considering that it's not unusual to find the odd sack of rice under a patient's bed or even the occasional chicken. The other day I was surprised to see a little boy pulling a bullock across the top end of the ward because he thought it was the quickest way to get from one side of the hospital to the other! Perhaps I haven't mentioned it before, but there isn't any glass in the windows! The metal window frames were put in place when the ward was extended some years ago, but the glass never arrived!

How to See a Hundred Men Before Lunch

Tomorrow will be Wednesday again and I'm always a little apprehensive about the Meherpur Clinic because there could be up to three hundred patients. As this is a Muslim town, Benny and I see the men at one end of the clinic and Florence sees the women at the other end with one of the nurses.

There's a bolted door between the consulting room and the waiting room. Ten patients are given a ticket with '*1*' on it, and the next ten have a ticket with '*2*', each further group of ten having the subsequent numbers, three, four and five, right up to a hundred patients. We methodically unbolt the door and shout, "*Number 1!*" and ten men rush into our room and sit on the benches around the walls, the floor and even on the windowsills. Quickly we heave against the door and lock it again. When we've dealt with the 'number ones', we unbolt the door and shout out, "*Number 2!*" and another ten men rush into the room. And so it goes on for hours, until the last patient has been seen. It reminds me of those passages in the Bible describing Jesus' Galilean ministry when the disciples were complaining that they were so busy that they didn't have time to eat! We must make the most of Benny's last three weeks here because, after that, I'll be on my own!

2 June Whit Sunday

Just say *"Fit"*

It has been a rainy week, no doubt because of all the prayers for rain and, although today is dry, the place seems very damp and the air heavy. But inside the house it's a little cooler. Praise the Lord for another happy week! I get so much satisfaction when our patients improve because the ultimate responsibility for their care rests with me and doesn't go any further.

We had another bad eclamptic on Thursday. I slept in the school room above the operating theatre and got up five times during the first night and four times the following night. I told *Kolpona,* one of our night nurses, not to bother with any Bengali preamble when she came to wake me. "*Just say FIT,*" I said, and that's just what she did! However, a super baby was born undamaged, and this morning the patient is coming out of her sedation and looks well on the way to recovery.

We've been listening to the World Service Radio a lot lately and it's been fun to listen to *Dad's Army* on Sunday nights, although the reception is only good for an hour or two at the most.

Now that the season of tomatoes, aubergines and beans is over, the food situation is looking a bit grim, there no longer being many vegetables to be found in the market. Someone sent a packet of dried peas through the post recently and we were thrilled!

A Visit to the Dentist

My holiday hasn't quite turned out as I'd originally planned. You'll remember that I had intended to go north to spend a week with Jack Praeger, my old college friend. Last week I discovered that his work had been closed down by the authorities and he'd gone back to Dublin. It was quite a disappointment because I had plans to fly there from *Jessore* and then to spend a week with Keith and Ruby in *Dhaka*. Instead, I went straight to *Dhaka,* where I stayed with Bishop James in the Old City.

Dhaka, what an indescribable place! I have never ever seen so many people: taxi drivers, rickshaws, beggars, cripples, children, shops lining every street, people shouting, hooting, ringing bells, dusty streets, Muslims chanting, people pulling huge cartloads of wood, cattle, chickens, crows everywhere and literally thousands of people walking through the streets. Stop anywhere for a moment and one is quickly surrounded by beggars with their hands out.

I had the opportunity of visiting a dentist and he set about removing the calculus that had built up around my lower teeth. I asked him why I accumulated so much. His answer was short and to the point: "*Because you talk too much*" he replied!

One evening, we went to the British Council to watch a film version of *The Merchant of Venice* and, on another, we were invited to the Deputy High Commissioner's home. It was filled with old maps and paintings of Monmouthshire in water colours and oils which made me a little homesick, of course. They are members of the church here in *Dhaka* and were very anxious to give us a splendid evening. It was a nice break from Bollobhpur although *Old Dhaka* is dusty, dirty, noisy and crammed with people.

Little Boys and Fruit Bats

It's now the fruit season – mangos, jackfruits and lychees are beginning to appear in the markets. Every year, the church council auctions the lychee trees in the churchyard, and whoever buys them takes on the responsibility of preventing the birds and the fruit bats from eating the fruit. So young boys sleep under the trees and rattle bamboo sticks and oil cans attached to ropes suspended high up in the branches. Every half an hour throughout the day and night they pull the ropes and rattle the sticks and tins. The noise is frightful, but the little boys (who are paid for this essential job) seem to have great fun and the poor fruit bats don't get anywhere near enough to eat the fruit. You sometimes see them flying over in the twilight. They can have a wingspan of two or three feet and are known to travel miles in search of food. Anyway it looks like there's a storm coming up, the wind is blowing and I can just hear the thunder in the distance, so I will end.

18 June

Monsoon

Well, it looks as if the monsoon season has arrived. It's been raining heavily on and off all day and the air is humid. Already the roads are churning up and it's unlikely that we're going to go to *Meherpur* tomorrow. Everything is already very damp, even down to the paper money in my wallet. So I've put my camera, pins and watch in a sealed tin to prevent the mould and I'm told they'll probably stay there till September!

Many thanks for your lovely letters and birthday card. I am writing to you at the grand old age of twenty-nine but I've never felt fitter. The *South Wales Argus* arrived a few days ago and, as usual, we all took great delight in reading it.

I've started to grow my beard again, having found that it is too painful to shave with blunt razor blades.

I'm so pleased that Tenovus has donated £100, and the pupils of the High School have sent £50. I've lost count of the number of gifts and donations that we have received in the short time that I have been here, everyone at home has been so generous. The gifts will be a big step forward for the hospital, because our new tetanus ward can now be fitted with metal frames and glass windows. The windows are ready for collection, and they should be fitted by July or August. Although exceedingly rare in England, tetanus claims many babies, children and adults over here and we are regularly admitting patients. It is the local custom to seal a new-born baby's umbilicus with cow dung, which results in countless neonatal deaths.

25 June

This week has been rather sad because of the imminent departure of Benny. Nobody could ask for a better friend, companion, and colleague. We shall all miss him.

We've had a new minor ops. room constructed out of the men's ward and it's looking great. There have been one or two heavy downpours yesterday, but I'm told there's worse to come. The air gets heavier every day but it doesn't bother me.

A Birthday Feast and Benny's Departure
My birthday coincided with Benny's farewell which has made it doubly memorable. Here follows a description of the day:

We had breakfast at 6.00 a.m. with cards and little presents from the community and two boiled eggs! Thence to church, after which we were invited to a feast with the nurses. This involved two sessions, sweets early in the morning, then the main meal at midday. They gave us so much in the first session: *roshagolas* (milk-based sweets boiled in sugar), sweet rice, yoghurt, jackfruit, mangos and pineapple, that we were absolutely bursting. Then we were given huge bouquets of wildflowers and lovely cards from the nurses. We collapsed back into bed and slept for the rest of the morning. Then at 12.30 p.m. we went back to the nurses' quarters for the main course – a curry with rice, *dhal*, spices and vegetables, all eaten (with our right hands) off banana leaves as we sat cross-legged on the floor. Most of the nurses ate with us, whilst the others piled up more and more rice and curry. We thanked the nurses so much for their generosity and hospitality – it's a very characteristic trait in the Bengalis. Lots of "*onek donabards*" were offered and we returned to the house.

Then followed an afternoon finishing off a sad book about the fate of the American Indians called *Bury My Heart in Wounded Knee*, followed by tea with a special cake baked by Lizzie. At 7.00 p.m. we all went down to Tom and Di's for a celebration meal for Benny, myself and the safe arrival of their baby girl, *Susila*. We finished off Tom's homemade beer. Then I drove the Land Rover back to Bollobhpur with everybody singing heartily in the back.

The celebrations were not over though, for last night the nurses put on some entertainment with songs and Indian dances and hilarious impromptu sketches. They are so elegant and dance beautifully with colourful saris and bells around their ankles. What a birthday! But of course, it's really sad that Benny is leaving. We shall all miss him so much.

2 July

Reducing a Dislocated Shoulder

I reduced a dislocated shoulder this morning for the first time using the proven method of putting my foot in the poor chap's armpit and pulling, although I'd never seen it done before. It clicked back in two seconds and both the patient and I were pleased with the result. A few weeks ago when we were all at *Meherpur*, except Lizzie, a patient came in with a dislocated jaw. After several attempts she couldn't reduce it. But when Florence came back, she put her thumbs firmly on the lady's back teeth, pulled down and pushed back and the jaw clicked back without a problem.

Otherwise, it's been a quiet day. People generally keep away at the beginning of the monsoon until they get used to its inconvenience. It's teeming with rain again now.

Please don't think I'm starving out here. The food is a bit monotonous and it would be a nice change to have something different occasionally. You can imagine how much pleasure we get from the odd tin of peas or an occasional packet of Angel Delight. Don't worry about my lack of money either because there is little or nothing to spend it on. I get a little pocket money – but generally speaking, the only money that passes through my hands from week to week is the church collection.

Last Friday I was stricken with a virus: a bad stomach and a temperature of 103. I felt rather poorly and had a few days in bed, but progressed rapidly and was fine again by Monday when I did two tubal ligations. My watch has broken again, so it's easy to lose touch with the time of day. This is the fourth time it's broken. Yes, the rains finally came yesterday 'good and proper', with a very heavy downpour all day. We rushed out and stood under the warm water gushing off the roof. It was the best shower I'd ever had and such a relief in this incredibly hot and humid climate, even though I was still wearing my clothes! Today everything is clean and the trees and buildings are dripping. There are puddles everywhere. Thank heavens for grandfather's Pakamac!

7 July Sunday

Farewell to Benny and Becky

Benny arrived back from *Dhaka* on Tuesday for his last night at Bollobhpur before leaving for home in South India. It's been disappointing that, having given a whole year of his career to the people of Bangladesh, he had so much trouble getting permission to leave. It's taken a fortnight trudging round the government offices in *Dhaka* and it's been quite a worry for him. His departure means that I will be the only doctor here but, believe me, I'm quite happy and confident. I know I'm getting extra strength from above.

Becky too is getting ready to fly home next week. She is rather sad and weepy. She's only eighteen and she's made many friends among the orphans and nurses. She has been a major help too. She oversaw all the sterilizing of equipment, gloves and gowns. As you can imagine the demand for sterilized instruments is constant. She's a super guitar player too. They will both go down to Calcutta, from thence to Madras, where Benny will start his new job and Becky will fly home to England. Eryl is going down to see them off and do some shopping.

Sold for Sixpence

It's Sunday afternoon again, with a full hospital, but it's quiet at the moment. We are looking forward to going across to the orphanage for an *utsob* (celebration tea) this afternoon. The invitation was brought by *Sunita*, a 13-year-old girl who was sold by her parents for six *poishas* when she was a baby. The rains are coming more frequently now. Every afternoon we have a heavy downpour, but everything dries out quickly and it's great to enjoy the cool breeze which accompanies the rain and makes sleeping at night a little more comfortable.

A Busy Wednesday

At *Meherpur* last Wednesday, I saw a hundred men before lunch, thirty to forty women in the early afternoon and came back to Bollobhpur as fresh as a daisy! I am doing more dentistry these days. I've discovered that one needs quite a lot of strength to extract teeth! An old gentleman returned a week after I had removed his painful tooth, still complaining of toothache. "*Didn't I take your tooth out last week?*" I asked. "*Yes,*" he replied, "*but you pulled the wrong one out!*" I'm quite certain I removed the one that he'd asked me to!

It continues to get stickier and stickier, but this afternoon it's cool in the house and soon I'll go and throw a couple of buckets of cold water over myself for a bit of refreshment. We went for a swim in the river on Sunday afternoon. It was deliciously cold. The villagers, who were washing their clothes, and the little boys scrubbing the family water buffalo, looked on amazed! We enjoyed the packet of soup immensely, so many thanks from all of us. It was a real treat. Well, I must stop now or Becky will have packed her case and there will be no room for my note.

10 July 6.10 p.m.

Florence Fractures Her Wrist

When Florence was going over to the hospital at 6.00 a.m. to see a *poati,* she slipped in the garden and fractured her wrist. It was a Colles fracture with a classic dinner-fork displacement. Unfortunately, she had to wait until I came back from *Meherpur* before I could set it under an anaesthetic. We'll retake the X-rays tomorrow and see if it has aligned well.

What a journey back from *Meherpur* with the Land Rover full of *rogies,* in addition to Pat, Eryl, myself and *Monju.* Now the rainy season has arrived, the roads are turning into quagmires with deep pools of water between the ridges left by bullock carts. But *Driver* somehow manages it, and, although we didn't travel much faster than ten miles an hour, we got back safely, the jeep slipping and sliding all over the road.

Now Florence's arm has been reduced, I've done a ward round and a D&C. I've thrown a few buckets of chilly water over myself and am now sitting here in the lamplight, happy and satisfied with a good day's work. Very many thanks for my birthday present of £4 which you have put into my bank account. Thank you ever so much because, as you can guess, that means a great deal to me these days.

12 July

It's hard to believe that I've been here nine months, the weeks fly past so quickly. I've found many blessings in Bollobhpur. The total involvement with patients, staff and villagers is so rewarding. In the past I've always wanted to be 'where the action is'. Well, I've discovered a new contentment in life – because the action is here! There is always such a lot going on, even the changes of season are quite dramatic. For instance, the beginning of the monsoon began only a week ago, but the roads are already impassable and we are more or less cut off. Yesterday it took over two hours to drive the ten miles to *Meherpur* through the mud and deep pools of water left by the wheels of the bullock carts.

14 July Sunday

A Ten Mile Walk in the Dark
It has been raining hard all morning and is pleasantly cool now. The goats are outside in the garden and they make a strange coughing noise from time to time. Bishop James is next door! He was expected yesterday, but when he hadn't turned up by sunset we thought he'd stayed at *Meherpur*, having already taken twelve hours to drive his Land Rover from *Dhaka,* and the road to Bollobhpur is now almost completely submerged in mud. To our surprise however, just as we were going to bed at 10.00 p.m., he arrived, covered in mud, his white cassock soaked with perspiration and stuck to him. He had walked the final ten miles from *Meherpur* in the dark with only a hurricane lamp. Behind him came his bearer carrying a suitcase on his head! Not bad for a seventy-year-old gentleman, wouldn't you say!

He was up bright and early before 7.00 a.m. to preach at Matins. His Bengali is clear and grammatical and I was pleased to discover that I understood almost all of his sermon. My own language improves day by day. To be able to speak another language fluently is quite a new experience. Some Bengali medical terms are very descriptive: they talk about "*chin chin*" to describe tingling in one's hands and feet, "*sum sum*" for a headache, "*bill bill*" for a nagging pain and, best of all, "*tog bog*" for indigestion!

Two other phrases seem to crop up quite often in conversations with the nurses: "*Ami chillam na*" ("I wasn't there!") and "*Ta horte pare kinto...*" ("That might be so but..."). It is often difficult to pin somebody down as to what may, or may not, have happened!

New Challenges

Things began to get busy again last week, and the beds were filled twice over. We have two serious tetanus cases at the moment but they should do alright given time. Another chap came in from the government hospital in *Meherpur* where they had treated a compound fracture of his arm by sticking a square of plaster of Paris over the exposed bone. Sadly, his arm was now grossly infected and gangrenous. I'm thinking of amputating his arm, but that's a big step, as I haven't done one before and have never seen one performed.

I was called out in the night to see a girl in obstructed labour. I attempted a manual rotation but she continued to labour in vain and I didn't think that it had been successful. I alerted the nurses to prepare for a caesarean section and was about to wake the others up to assist me, but to everyone's delight the girl delivered spontaneously twenty minutes later. My manoeuvre seemed to have done the trick and I hadn't realised it! Anyway, the nurses made us all a cup of very sweet tea which we drank in the darkness of the ward with just a flickering of the paraffin lamp to see by, and I finally got back to bed at 2.00 a.m.

By the way, the repeat X-Ray of Florence's wrist showed a good position following the reduction, so she should be alright when the plaster comes off in six weeks' time. I'm writing rather a lot of medical stuff this week and do hope you're not bored by it all.

Unusual Names

The orphans gave us a concert last week. We sat on the grass for two hours while they performed dances, songs and little sketches. All ages were involved, from fourteen-year-olds down to little three-year-old tots. It was delightful, so graceful when you think how English children of the same age would have plodded around.

I had a good sleep this afternoon and woke up to the sound of hymn-singing coming across from the church. Then we had a slice of Lizzie's banana cake for tea. We sat on the steps at the front of the house and I cradled a little three-month-old orphan in my arms. Her name was *Sandhya* because she had *'arrived in the evening'*.

They choose interesting names here: I've heard of a little boy called *'Helicopter'* because a helicopter flew over the village on the day that he was born, and they talk of another unfortunate child who was given a Bengali name which, translated into English, means *'throw him in the fireplace!'* Still, if you've already got a dozen children, I suppose you begin to run out of names.

Early News of the Second Coming

Dinner was a very pleasant one, as Bishop James is great company and has a fund of anecdotes. He tells the story of how he and his colleague, Bishop Michael, were waiting in Calcutta for the arrival of a third bishop whose name was Christopher. They finally received a telegram, advising that the visitor had been delayed. The telegram should have read: "*Coming tomorrow,*" signed "*Christopher*". But the Indian Post Office (which is renowned for making small errors) had left off the last five letters of the message, so that it now read: "*Coming tomorrow,*" signed "*Christ.*" "My goodness," said Bishop Michael to Bishop James, "You *are* privileged!"

We usually sit out on the steps after dinner under the stars to keep cool, sometimes playing Scrabble or listening to the radio. Tonight it was raining hard, so we sat inside and had a cup of tea in the dining room. It's now 10.00 p.m. and I'm back in the bungalow. It's getting humid again and I can hear the noise of the crickets and the croaking bullfrogs all around. I'm just about to say my prayers and climb under my mosquito net.

19 July Friday

Thank you for the *South Wales Argus* which arrived safely. I notice that there was a paragraph about me in the paper. But it should really have been about those marvellous kids at the High School having raised another £50.

The other evening, as we sat out on the veranda, we started asking each other: "*Where would you like to go tomorrow?*" Lizzie usually says "*Brighton*", Eryl says "*London*" and I say "*Stratford*"!

As I'm writing this letter, I have a towel wrapped around my feet because the mosquitoes are terrible at this time of night. I'm surprised at this intermittent rain. I always thought that the monsoon rains would be persistent, but the heavy downpours come only for a few hours at a time; even so, the river is rising rapidly. We worry about the increasing slope on the back lawn that overlooks the river. It has dropped by a foot over the last couple of years and the villagers wonder whether the mission house will still be here in five years' time.

A Difficult Amputation

I had a busy afternoon amputating that poor chap's arm. It took three hours and it was a difficult job. He was noticeably big and had an excellent blood supply! Lizzie was assisting, Eryl anaesthetising, Pat was scrub nurse and *Monju* was constantly wiping my forehead so that sweat wouldn't drip down onto the patient. I couldn't have had better help. We have no diathermy here, so we used ninety swabs. You can imagine how much bleeding there was. When we had finished at 4.30 p.m. I was soaked through with perspiration. It was exhausting and backbreaking work, leaning over the table for so long. The man is well, thank God. I think he will be alright as long as the ligatures don't slip.

We're all looking forward to a nice dinner and a quiet evening so that we can recover enough energy to go to *Meherpur* tomorrow and see two hundred patients! You see, you need such patience and humility there. Sometimes it can be frustrating beyond belief, with dozens of people shouting in a different language, much of which you don't understand. How Jesus managed to cope even when they had to lower a chap through a hole in the roof because the room was so crowded, I don't know! I admire him for his patience. The light from the oil lamp is fading slowly, so I must bring this letter to a close. Florence's fractured wrist is healing well.

I found this lovely prayer yesterday: *"O Lord, save us from anxiety, and if we **are** anxious, let us commit ourselves more fully to you; and, this day, may we be able to do some work of peace for you."*

25 July

Learning the Language

My *Bangla* (Bengali) is slowly improving and I find that these days I'm pretty well able to communicate with the patients and the villagers. The nurses laugh at me sometimes, but they are really helpful, speaking slowly and carefully, so that I can understand. I was not surprised to hear that the Bengali language shares its origins with some other Indo-European languages. So 'mother' is translated as *ma,* 'name' is translated as *nam* and there are many other similarities. Of course, we have borrowed several words back from Bengali, such as *char, chitty, tiffin, chutney* and so on.

The number of outpatients I see each day is enormous, sometimes up to a hundred men, women or children. After all that talking in a foreign language, I'm glad to sit down in the evenings and read, as there is little else to do. We enjoy listening to the radio too. I'm learning just to be happy by myself as well. I'm sure God helps us through the difficult times, the bad cases and the occasional moments of loneliness in this isolated place.

We got stuck badly on the way to *Meherpur* on Wednesday. We were quickly surrounded by men who appeared from the village, all trying to dig the jeep out of the deep mud. We finally got it free, only to get it stuck again a mile or so down the road. After about two hours we had only managed to get two miles out of Bollobhpur and decided that we'd never get to the clinic. So Florence, Pat, Lizzie and I walked back to the hospital and had a nice cup of tea. I was grateful for the rest, as Wednesday is a quiet day here in Bollobhpur and it gave me time to recover from another busy week. I was soon fine again and raring to go. The chap whose gangrenous arm I amputated last week is doing well and we're hoping for a rapid recovery.

30 July

Eye Surgery and the Pleasure of a Boiled Sweet

I'm sitting on the back veranda, a nice cool evening with my feet up on the table to avoid the mosquitoes, listening to the birds. There is someone playing a pipe a little way down the river. The sky is cloudy and pink with dark clouds on the distant eastern horizon. Directly across the river the fields are full of jute, which are leafy green plants about six-foot high and will be harvested in a few weeks' time. At long last the water hyacinth, which has covered the river in both directions for the last three months, is beginning to move downstream carried along by the rising level of the river. Since the roads are now impassable, tomorrow we will set out for *Meherpur* by boat! It means an early start at 5.00 a.m. and the boatman will row us down the river in about three or four hours. Hopefully, we will arrive there to begin the clinic at about 8.30 a.m. It should be a pleasant journey through the countryside as it wakes up to a fresh morning.

It's now 10.00 p.m. and another evening has gone! I was going to settle down to write to you after dinner, but, as usual, there was something else to do. A chap was admitted with an eye injury after something exploded in the fire. So I've been sewing his eyelids until now! It was rather an intricate job as everything was done on such a small scale, but it seemed to come together alright. I think that he's lost the sight of his eye as there was an internal penetrating wound, about which we could do little.

I'm sitting here in the lamplight with a cup of coffee and a boiled sweet. It's funny to think a boiled sweet could be such a treat. Please don't be anxious about any news of floods that may be reaching you. There *are* floods in Bangladesh, but they are two hundred miles south and our location is too elevated to be affected by them. I must go to bed now or I'll never get up in the morning.

God is so good. He gives me strength and patience every day. I feel Him around me all the time.

3 August Saturday

A Successful Attempt to Reach *Meherpur* by River

You may remember that last Wednesday we were hoping to get to *Meherpur* by boat, so, trusting that the river had cleared of water hyacinth, I was woken at 4.30 a.m. We had breakfast just as it was getting light and at about 5.30 a.m., we boarded the boat which had been brought round to the bank alongside the churchyard. What a squeeze it was: with Florence and Pat, *Togor,* Solomon (a young man from the village who gives out the tickets and takes the cash) and *Driver*, together with all the boxes of drugs.

The trip was pleasant! I dozed on and off as we slipped down the river, the brilliant colours of the sky changing minute by minute with only the sound of the birds and the splash of the oars breaking the silence of the morning. Soon the hot sun rose higher and we sheltered from its heat under umbrellas. Sometimes there was just thick undergrowth on the bank, but in most places, we passed little communities waking up, the villagers washing themselves and their clothes, while others had already started to fish.

But in many places the weed was still thick, stretching across the river, which, for most of its length, is not much wider than the Avon at Stratford. Our journey took five hours. We arrived at 10.20 a.m. and found the place milling with patients, more than usual because we hadn't made it the week before. I quickly got started on the men and saw about a hundred and twenty of them by 4.00 p.m., having taken a half-hour break at lunch time. Florence and Pat got through the women at an equal rate. Then followed a cup of tea and a cake, a ward round which included a chase to get a marauding chicken out from under one of the beds, and finally we set off across the two fields behind the hospital to the boat moored at the bank.

It was now raining so we all crammed under the cover and were soon underway. The sky was as colourful as it was at sunrise, with dark rain clouds in the distance and even a rainbow. About three and a half miles outside Bollobhpur we found that the weed was too thick to navigate and the boat could go no further, so we decided to walk.

By now it was dark and drizzly, but soon the rain cleared and a full moon came up to light our path through the clusters of mud houses that we passed along the way. Here and there we saw little pools of light from hurricane lamps and heard the sounds of evening village life, children chattering and singing, young boys reciting their school lessons and distant conversations around family fires. Because the way was muddy and slippery, Florence was terrified that she might slip and re-fracture her arm. We stumbled barefoot through the mud and finally reached Bollobhpur at 9.15 p.m., having started out at dawn. Eryl had a meal waiting for us and I went to bed tired and happy.

The days go by so quickly! Tom, Di and the new baby are on their way to *Chittagong* for their holiday. I thought I'd write my weekly epistle a day earlier so that they can take it with them when they go.

The X-ray Department
We are extremely lucky to have X-ray facilities right out here in the middle of nowhere, though the machine functions only intermittently. The results do help a lot when we have them. Lizzie has gone to the Christian hospital at *Chandraghona* on the east side of the country to learn some more about taking and interpreting X-rays. She produces excellent images on the few occasions when the generator is working. Interpreting them is often a problem though – fractured arms and legs are quite easy to read, but chests and abdomens sometimes baffle us, as you can imagine. Anyway, when Lizzie comes back, she'll be able to tell us lots more about radiology.

Floods and Relief
We heard on the BBC last night that Bangladesh has appealed for relief because of the floods in other parts of the country but, thank heavens, they are miles away from us. The Ganges flows south from the Himalayas through Bangladesh, firstly passing through *Assam*, which is reputed to be the wettest place on earth. Every year the rivers rise to danger point, but thankfully the floods don't come this

far west and we are on slightly higher ground anyway. In fact, the last two or three days have been dry and cool, rather like a bright December day at home. The river is rising slowly and in the last twenty-four hours it has taken all the water hyacinth downstream. It flows by so gently, reminding me of Stratford on a sunny day! You expect to see the odd pleasure boat or a swan passing by at any moment!

I'm a little sceptical about the British government's appeal for more disaster relief funds. We hear that there are areas of Bangladesh which are experiencing a food shortage at the moment but we do not appear to be affected, though the price of rice has risen sharply. I'm sorry to say that it would seem that only little of what is donated by the developed countries gets through to the poor people here, for much of it is diverted into the pockets of wealthy politicians and their Swiss bank accounts. Bangladesh's biggest obstacle to progress is not natural disasters but corruption. My advice to anyone who wants to give money for relief is to give it through organisations such as Save the Children or Christian Aid.

Pat is going home to Bristol in two weeks' time for a well-earned break. She will soon begin visiting churches all over the country and talking about her work here. She loves working in the operating theatre and is a tremendous help to me in the big operations. She is a marvellous singer and a great mimic.

I'm told that, locally, it has been exceptionally dry for this time of the year and yet we hear increasing news of flooded areas around *Dhaka*. It's rather hard to believe because so many official reports on the local radio are just untrue. We heard that the floods were worsening in *Kushtia*, with *Meherpur* under six foot of water. Yet we were there at the hospital last week and there was no sign of the river overflowing the banks. It would seem that these local reports are just attempts to divert relief money from the capital! We did, however, catch the tail end of a cyclone centred in the Indian Ocean last week with twelve hours of high winds, but the weather is fine again now. No damage was done and we were glad of a breather.

Midnight Surgery

Wednesday proved to be another long one. I was up at 4.30 a.m. to take the boat to *Meherpur*. We got back by 8.15 p.m. and I hoped to get an early night by going to bed at 10.00 p.m. At midnight, however, I was called to see a woman in obstructed labour and decided that a caesarean section was necessary. Everyone got up for the operation, which went well, and I got back to bed at 5.30 a.m. The circumstances were sad though. This young girl had already had two still-births, and if she had another one the husband was liable to throw her out, as is common practice here. The unborn baby was again in trouble and the only chance to save it was by doing a caesar, but we operated in vain, for the baby was stillborn despite our efforts. Now the husband will most probably discard her: "*It's cheaper to buy a new wife than to pay for an operation*," they say.

Life is sad.

With love and prayers.

25 August Sunday

The Prayer of St. Francis

Lord, make me an instrument of your peace. Where there is hatred, let me sow love; where there is injury, pardon; where there is doubt, faith; where there is despair, hope, where there is darkness, light; where there is sadness, joy. O Lord, grant that I may not so much seek to be consoled as to console, not so much to be understood as to understand, not so much to be loved, as to love. For it is in giving that we receive; it is in pardoning that we are pardoned; and it is in dying that we wake to eternal life.

I've come across this prayer again recently. When I was at Saint Mary's Hospital in Tucson, USA, it was read out over the tannoy each morning and all the nurses, porters, and doctors would stop to listen to its beautiful words in silence. Then I lost the words for several years, until I heard it again at Niall and Sue's wedding when they read it together at the end of their service. Several summers ago, when I met them again, I said how fond I was of it and they gave me their own copy of the prayer. A year later a friend of mine was in great despair and I gave that copy to her, hoping that she might find it as helpful as I had done. So again I lost the words until I came to *Barisal* and found the prayer was known by a Canadian girl at the language school there. Recently, here in Bollobhpur, I found a book called *Instrument of Thy Peace* by Alan Peyton, the anti-apartheid activist. In the introduction he writes that whenever he prayed this prayer his melancholy was dispelled, his self-pity ended and his faith restored. I hope that you will love the words as thousands of people across the world already do.

3 September

It's very hot and humid here today. As I'm writing to you I am having to rest my hand on a handkerchief to stop the letter getting soaking wet. Now I've dropped my pen on the floor and spoiled the nib!

Florence celebrated her 60th birthday on Sunday. We had a birthday feast prepared by the nurses at lunchtime sitting on mats eating pumpkin, rice and *tarkari*, which is a vegetable curry. It was a good job that we could have a snooze in the afternoon! The evening's entertainment included dances and songs beautifully performed by the nurses, who tied bells around *our* ankles and encouraged us to join in. It was great fun.

"Praying is Love on its Knees"
I've been reading a book about how, through prayer, we can become part of God's work in the world. When one prays, coincidences happen! Despite a chronic shortage of supplies, we never seem to be prevented from giving a drug or anaesthetic when they are needed. So many of my decisions turn out to be the right ones even though I'm sure I have neither the skill nor the knowledge to make them; so many of our patients get better although we wouldn't have expected them to. We seem to cope, no matter what happens; we are content to live in such an isolated place month after month, with nothing but books and the occasional wireless programme to occupy the evening hours. I am certain that many people are praying for us because God helps so much in all this. I was never much good at praying before I

went to bed, because I was always too sleepy, but I try now to pray early in the evening, not only for what is going on here, but also for the whole world. It's giving me such happiness to do so. *'Praying is love on its knees,'* someone wrote.

8 September

Safe Delivery of a Goat

Last week I delivered an obstructed goat which had been brought to the hospital by one of the villagers. I'm glad to report that both the mother, the kid and the obstetrician are doing well! Thank goodness all was successful because the goat was of great value.

Many thanks for your parcel containing packets of Angel Delight and a cheese mix! I'm looking forward enormously to the latter on toast, especially if we can find an egg to put on top of it – that would be pure bliss!

Another super week has passed at Bollobhpur, filled with professional satisfaction and new spiritual insights. In fact, I have never been so healthy, rested and happy. The total involvement in this place is beyond anything I could have imagined. The work does not seem to be the least bit too overwhelming. It's quite true that we *are* given strength to cope. Only Lizzie and Eryl and myself are here at the moment but not even the heavy clinics are daunting and I find that I can face all-comers and all situations with a relaxed and peaceful mind. The work may be challenging, but I have the long evenings to recuperate. We sit out on the steps under the stars reading by hurricane lamp. I've just finished *Pride and Prejudice* and enjoyed it very much.

12 September

I'm looking forward to my holiday, leaving on Thursday the 19th, travelling to Calcutta and staying at the Oxford Mission until the 23rd. Then I'm flying down to South India to stay with Benny at *Vellore* where his father is Professor of Medicine. I'm hoping to attend the Christian Medical Association of India Conference, which begins on the 29th. It will be wonderful to be with other medics again, sharing problems and getting advice. Then I hope to spend a few days up in the hills at Bangalore Theological College with Cecil Hargreaves. From there I will fly back to Calcutta hoping to be back at Bollobhpur by the 7th.

We hear on the World Service that there is going be another general election at home. Too late for a postal vote, I guess, but anyway this time round I would have found it more difficult to know exactly which party to vote for.

I am sending this letter off to you by bullock cart and hope that it gets safely to the post office.

15 September

It's been a quiet week in the hospital. The large outpatient clinics continue as crowded and noisy as ever, the consultations interspersed with tubal ligations, abscesses and medical emergencies. I'm extracting a lot of teeth these days – the word must have got around! The monsoon is the worst time of the year for tropical diseases, so from that point of view, patient numbers should begin to ease a little as we look forward to the cooler days. There's no sign of cholera in the district, but we've all had booster inoculations as a precaution. They say we're having an unusual September, cloudy and cool, and soon there will be a need for a blanket at night. I'm sorry to hear that you've had a bad summer in England.

As I explained in my last letter, I have plans to go to South India next week and see some temples, mountains and jungles. How lucky I am!

24 September Tuesday

Christian Medical College, *Vellore*, South India
I am writing this letter in the college library. My visa eventually came through and I left Bollobhpur early on Thursday morning. The border officials were impressed by my *Bangla* and I was offered

sweet tea and biscuits. We had a chat about Shakespeare, Stratford and England and I thought I would miss the train, but it was late arriving as usual. As I waited on the platform I soon had a crowd of people around me and could have started a clinic right there and then! The two-hour journey to Calcutta was crammed with country people going to market: piles of bananas, baskets of fruit, beggars, babies, dust, and noise. We had quite a jolly time altogether!

Thence to the Oxford Mission Fathers to spend a quiet weekend at *Behala,* south of the city. The OMF is a community of Anglican Benedictines praying throughout the day at three hourly intervals and observing the 'great silence' between 9.00 p.m. and 9.00 a.m. This meant that I experienced my first silent breakfast, beckoning to one another whenever we needed to pass the marmalade. A great sense of peace and dedication pervades the mission. The Fathers were extremely interested in our work in Bollobhpur and invited me to return to *Behala* in the future. I think they were hoping that they might have gained a future novice for the Order.

The monks run a large boys' school, which is really fantastic; the pupils are happy, polite and friendly. In one quarter of the playing field there was cricket practice going on and in another a troop of Boy Scouts was gathering; in the school hall, young musicians were rehearsing for a concert. So strong is the musical tradition at *Behala* that one of the sixteen-year-old pupils has recently obtained a scholarship to study the cello at the Royal College of Music in London. The whole school seemed to be filled with activity whilst, in the beautiful chapel, psalms were being chanted throughout the day. On Sunday morning, many boys took part in a Eucharist which was set to stunning Indian music accompanied by drums and cymbals. In the evening, at a concert of Indian songs and music given in my honour, I was asked to contribute an item and sang a Gilbert and Sullivan song which was much appreciated. What wonderful Christian saints I met there in such a short time, elderly Anglican monks whose eyes sparkled with joy as you talked to them. Altogether a peaceful and restful weekend before I continued my journey.

Home visit.

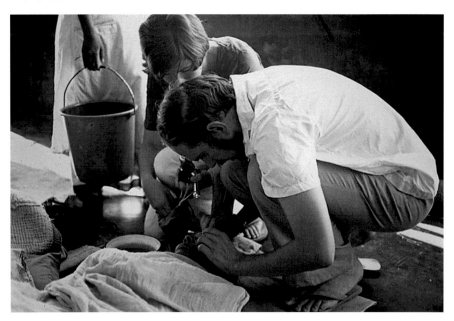

Eighty post-cataract patients to check.

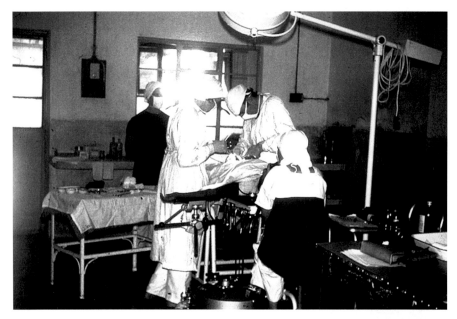

Operating by reflected sunlight.

Just a few more to see in Meherpur.

Waiting for an appointment.

Early start to Meherpur Hospital.

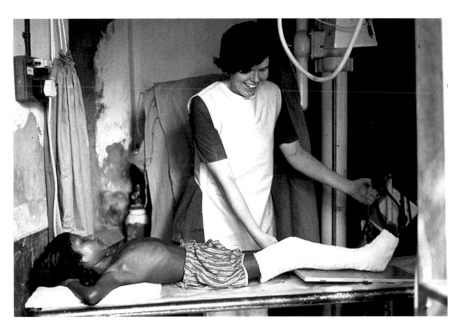

Lizzie prepares to take an X-Ray.

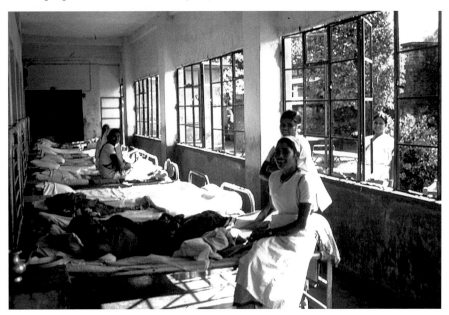

No glass in the windows.

Some of the Bollobhpur nurses.

Son Kerton band.

Long wait for ladies outpatients.

Newly acquired marbles.

Bullock carts in the hospital compound.

South to Madras and *Vellore*

On Monday I took a taxi to the airport and an easy flight took me eight hundred miles south to Madras Airport where Benny was waiting for me. As you can guess we had a great deal of catching up to do. The city has wide clean roads and fabulous shops, with shrines and gods looming up out of nowhere. But there were many Christian churches too since St. Thomas is said to have visited there after Jesus' Resurrection. Another two hours on a train (so crowded that there were even people lying on the luggage racks above us) brought us to *Vellore* where we finally arrived at Benny's home at 10.00 p.m. His father is Professor of Preventive Medicine and his mother is a lecturer in the Physiology Department, at present studying the effect of snake venom on dogs. They live on the campus. Benny has two lovely sisters, one of whom is a medical student.

This huge and bustling teaching hospital has a thousand beds and employs many doctors, nurses and supporting staff. A missionary lady founded it seventy years ago. The following morning, I was given a guided tour around this enormous complex, visiting a new surgical block of fourteen theatres where major surgery was being performed. I met a CMS missionary doctor working as an anaesthetist. She came from Cardiff and was momentarily staggered when I said I came from Newport! All the surgeons were pleasant and welcoming, showing me around and discussing their work. How our surgeons at home could learn lessons in politeness and friendliness! I'm sitting in the library and waiting for Benny to return from a lecture. What a revelation this has been, to be here in India, observing both its up-to-date technology and its ancient culture. How marvellous it is to be able to broaden one's mind so.

3 October

The Conference

What an enjoyable time I had with Benny's hospitable and generous family, but, all too soon my time at *Vellore* was over and I returned on a crowded train to Madras. I was met by Benny's father, who had already arrived for the conference. He had found me a pleasant hotel and took me out to dinner. Such kindness! I am overwhelmed by the trouble everyone has taken on my behalf.

The conference of two hundred and fifty delegates began with communion – a moving experience. The theme of the conference was *'The Healing Church'* and the next three days were filled with lectures and group discussions covering both its spiritual and medical aspects. I learned a great deal, sharing many problems and experiences with doctors and nurses of all nationalities. It was great to be able to say, *"What do you do with such and such a case?"* I was going to buy a skin-grafting knife, but it was too expensive so will have to continue to make do with an old-fashioned cut-throat razor. We ate splendid South Indian food served on banana leaves whilst chatting to surgeons, theologians and engineers. I met several other CMS folks, including an engineer, an anaesthetist, a pharmacist and an occupational therapist. We had a lovely evening together.

Bangalore

I left the conference a day early to travel to Bangalore – a five-hour journey by train which climbed steadily through granite passes and wooded valleys, away from the sweltering flat coastal plain and into the cool air and blue skies of the hills – to stay with another CMS couple, Cecil Hargreaves and his wife. They were kindness itself. Bangalore is a lovely, modern, clean city with glass-fronted shops! I took a day's tour to see the fabulous temples of South India and the Maharajah's palaces in *Mysore*. We travelled through the hills and mountains, with boulders everywhere. One particular temple was breathtaking, having been built out of solid rock. Six hundred and fifty steps were cut into the mountain, ascending to a temple courtyard constructed around the feet of a huge fifty-seven-foot statue of the Hindu god *Shiva* stretching right up into the sky. I was absolutely staggered. There were many other temples in the area, the exteriors covered with exquisite carvings, the insides filled with statues of gods in deep dark recesses and garlanded with flowers. They were rather creepy.

Back in Bangalore I went to the cinema one evening; the film was *If It's Wednesday, It Must Be Belgium!* We sat on benches and, every time the projector broke down, there was uproar amongst the enthusiastic audience.

8 October Tuesday

Prawns and Good Advice at the Victoria Hotel, Madras

You wouldn't believe where I have ended up! I left Bangalore yesterday, returning to Madras as planned, in plenty of time to catch the flight to Calcutta. But ten minutes before the plane took off we were informed that the flight had been indefinitely cancelled and we were escorted back to a first-class hotel in the city where we spent the night by courtesy of Indian airlines. Well, what a place! A really super hotel, a single room with air conditioning (heaven) and toilet paper! Everything was clean and the sheets crisp. Last night, I ate well on prawns and steak. An additional pleasure was the advice given by the management not to tip the porters, which is a blessing as one gets terribly miserable forever coping with beggars, taxi drivers and waiters, all trying to squeeze every last *taka* out of you.

We were supposed to fly to Calcutta this morning, but there is still no news from the airport so I'm making the most of this pleasant surprise ending to my holiday, enjoying the cleanliness and coolness of it all because it's blisteringly hot outside. I had intended to get all the hospital shopping done in Calcutta today: butter, cooking oil and medical supplies such as anaesthetic and catgut. If the plane isn't too late, there is a chance that I'll get it done this evening. The problem is that I must catch the 6.15 a.m. train from Calcutta tomorrow morning to meet *Driver* on the other side of the border who will have driven the Land Rover sixty miles south to meet me. Still, in the meantime, let's just enjoy it.

13 October Sunday

Back to Bollobhpur

My unexpected stay in the Victoria Hotel, Madras, concluded with bacon and eggs for breakfast. Praise the Lord! I couldn't help chuckling to myself as I demolished toast, marmalade, and coffee. The plane finally left Madras and we arrived in Calcutta at 5.15 p.m. It took another hour to get into the city from the airport and then I had to start shopping in New Market for groceries, drugs, writing paper, batteries, etc. I found the room where I had intended to stay but, unfortunately, it was locked and the Reverend *Daz* had taken the keys on holiday with him. So, loaded with provisions and luggage, I struggled to the Salvation Army Hostel to spend a night being annoyed by mosquitoes. It was made bearable, however, by the fact that the night was short and I had to get up at 5.30 a.m. to catch a train from Sealda Station north to the border.

Faithful *Driver* was waiting for me on the Bangladeshi side of the border and we had a good journey back to Bollobhpur where I found that Florence, Lizzie and Eryl had been having a tough time trying to cope without a doctor.

Over these last few weeks, I have met several students and young people travelling around the world. They all seemed rather tired, sad and envious of my work in Bangladesh. Most of them appeared to really want to be doing some good but couldn't settle anywhere, as a result of which they wandered aimlessly around the East.

An Acute Abdomen and a Confirmation Service

When I started to work again on Thursday, it turned out to be a particularly busy day with an acute appendix and an abnormal delivery as well as the men's clinic with over a hundred turning up. Having been away for three weeks, my nerves were a bit relaxed and it took a while to get back up to speed, but I quickly got into the swing of it and I'm coping alright again now.

Bishop James is here. He held a confirmation service yesterday for thirty boys and girls, mostly from the orphanage. The service was beautiful and his talk was simple. Once again, I was pleased to be able to understand his Bengali, making a change from many sermons that we sit through not understanding much at all because of the speed with which they are delivered.

On Friday afternoon we had a picnic at *Rotnapur* for the twenty orphans who hadn't gone back to relatives for the holidays. They went early in Tom's boat and we went down later in the bishop's Land Rover. We had great fun playing football with the children afterwards. Despite the fact that the roads are slowly getting back to normal, we got stuck in the mud on the way back and I ended up lying underneath the jeep trying to dig the wheel out.

I left England a year ago today on the 7.00 a.m. plane to Amsterdam!

20 October

Another hot and sticky Sunday afternoon but a nice feeling that the cooler weather is on the way. In fact, on one or two mornings last week, there was the faintest suggestion of an autumn nip in the air. According to Tom's records it's still about 95 during the day and very humid. I made several attempts to write to you this morning but firstly I found an ants' nest under my bed and spent twenty minutes washing it away, and then there were twins to deliver. I wrote a letter to Keith and Ruby because it was our first anniversary of arriving in Bangladesh together, and when I'd finished it was lunchtime.

We have an American girl staying with us from the National Council of Churches in *Dhaka*. She's actively involved in the Christian Health and Family Planning projects, as we are. She went off with Florence after lunch to visit some of the local villages. Florence is flying to Nepal at the end of the week to attend a conference. She will be glad of a rest and a change of scenery.

Lizzie has been unwell having got herself very anaemic and miserable, but we gave her an iron infusion on Thursday and we're hoping she'll soon be better. Meg has decided to stay in England for a year while she is making up her mind about the future. We will pray that she has clear guidance and peace of mind.

Festivals, Mosquitos and a Difficult Operation

It's been the Muslim festival of *Eid* this week, so the numbers at the clinics have been fewer. I always love the clinics anyway regardless of how many people turn up, as long as one can keep a bit of order and not have fifty people in the room at the same time.

Yesterday, we admitted a man with a perforated gangrenous appendix which I removed with difficulty. He was very ill indeed with peritonitis and I didn't think he'd survive, but today he's sitting up in bed and asking whether he can eat rice.

I've been getting some early nights lately. It's still too hot to sit indoors, but when we are out on the steps we are troubled by mosquitos. So having been bitten half a dozen times, I usually retire to bed under the mosquito net.

Fancy, it's only seven weeks to Christmas again. Where has the year gone!

27 October

The cooler weather has arrived! After a terrific storm on Tuesday it has finally cooled down a lot. There is a very pleasant breeze blowing through the window in front of me and we are naturally making the most of it. It has been an unusually hot October and I've suffered from prickly heat. Last week was busy but fulfilling, thank the Lord. Our appendix man is fine despite his near fatal condition when we operated. The stitches came out yesterday. He's wandering about wanting to eat curry and asking when he can go home.

Friday followed the usual busy pattern, beginning with a ward round, then a couple of sterilizations, followed by women's outpatients. At 11.45 a.m. a lady was admitted in obstructed labour and her condition merited preparing for a caesarean section. We all ran round in circles whilst awaiting permission to operate from her husband and family who lived three miles away over the fields. When all the preps had been made, I re-examined the lady and no caesar was necessary after all! After one or two procedures, the baby was born safely twenty minutes afterwards!

A short while later, when I was having a nap, someone came rushing over from the hospital – a young man had gashed his leg badly and was losing a lot of blood. Just as I was finishing suturing him up, another *poate* was admitted and there followed a difficult forceps. It was getting darker and darker and increasingly difficult to see what I was doing, but the girls brought in a hurricane lamp just before the baby was born. A super day – but we don't get many quite as hectic as that!

Eryl and Lizzie

Eryl is hoping to do a health visitor's course at Southampton University when she returns in July. They posted her entrance exam out here and asked me to invigilate. So yesterday she spent two hours sitting the examination whilst I sat in the room next door making sure she didn't cheat! We've had a lot of laughs about it. I'm sure she will do very well. She's a very clever girl.

Lizzie is better than she was, health-wise, and is rushing around doing a hundred things as usual. She loves doing mending jobs: electricity, machines, stethoscopes, pens that don't work, watches. She has a knack of making things work but she can't *spell* for nuts! We think she must be dyslexic. Apparently, her father is just the same. He's a successful inventor and runs his own family firm but she says *he* can't spell either!

Food prices are going up all round and everyone is wondering what will happen next. The fridge runs off kerosene (paraffin) as do the hurricane lamps, but it was in such a short supply last week that we were on the brink of having to use candles. Still, candlelight is soft on the eyes.

3 November

A Chilly Return from *Meherpur*

What a pleasure it is that the cooler weather has come at last! Although the sun is still extremely hot during the day there is a most delightful cool breeze around the place and the humidity is rapidly diminishing. It's difficult to describe how pleasant it is to have our meals out on the veranda again and afterwards to sit in the wicker chairs and drink tea whilst looking down over the river. The countryside on the other side of the river is looking green, fresh and beautiful. We can't help smiling and saying, *"Isn't this beautiful, just like summer at home"* and we're trying to make the most of it. At night sheets will be needed from now on because the temperature drops rapidly after dark. On one occasion last week, I even needed a blanket!

Last Wednesday at *Meherpur*, after a busy clinic followed by a ward round, we returned on the boat. By 6.00 p.m. it was dark and a most beautiful full moon rose in a clear starlit sky. It was a lovely trip sitting huddled under patchwork blankets and singing songs as we drifted past a lone fisherman on the banks and little groups of houses lit only by flickering fires and the odd oil lamp here and there. From both banks, we heard the noise of domesticity as the men came home from the fields, the evening meals were being prepared, children played and dogs barked.

We've had a chap called Bryan staying with us this weekend. He's a VSO, who has come to *Rotnapur* to assist Tom at the intermediate technology school there. He's a cheery twenty-four-year-old engineer from Kingston on Thames and we had a hilarious game of Monopoly last night. We hope that, after dinner tonight, we'll have a game of gin rummy, but there's no electricity and the lamps are a bit dim. One can't do very much after dark, but that doesn't deter us. Lizzie has been busy cooking and Eryl has taken part in the hospitality too. Florence remains in *Kathmandu* until next week.

Successes and Failures

It's been a mixed week medically. Soon after church on Sunday morning I did my rounds and was pleased to find that everyone was either getting better or awaiting discharge. The appendix man is remarkably well. I cannot account for it.

Unfortunately, we had a sixteen-year-old girl who died in labour yesterday. Thank heavens we see only a few maternal deaths despite the appalling conditions. But when one *does* occur, we are always extremely sad. We worked hard all Saturday morning from 5.30 a.m. till 2.00 p.m. to save her, but this poor girl had been in an ox cart for twenty-four hours, convulsing on her way to us. We feel we did our best and that is most important. The traditional wailing that accompanies a death, with people throwing themselves on the ground, is very distressing.

Tetanus

Another hour was spent yesterday trying to persuade a man to admit his son who was suffering from the dreadful spasms of tetanus. The villagers are often so foolish and won't let their children be admitted. The more the nine-year-old boy cried and got distressed, the more spasms he had. The father kept on asking the boy whether he wanted to be admitted which made him even more distressed. Eventually, using my strongest Bengali, I persuaded the father to admit his son. Soon the lad was well sedated and under cool sheets. This morning he has improved a lot and I have great hopes for his recovery.

Many thanks for your lovely letters accompanied by the occasional *South Wales Argus* and delightful packets of soup. As usual, we downed the soup with great pleasure – and the cheese sauce was out of this world! Everyone sends their thanks for your thoughtfulness.

I'm sorry that my letters may change in style from week to week but often the mood of the letter depends on the atmosphere of hope or despair, anxiety or relief, that prevails at the time of writing.

Please don't worry about sending me any money, as I have sufficient cash for my needs. I use the pocket money that I get from the hospital to buy razor blades or a book whenever somebody goes to *Dhaka* or Calcutta, but most of the time, we don't go anywhere near a shop, so the money mounts up quite quickly. I would not have much use of a bank account, anyway, as the nearest bank is a hundred miles away.

Recalling Past Meals

We often think of home and we talk about our families and friends constantly. We re-live great meals of the past and imagine bottles of wine. We remember visits to the theatre and cinema. We share memories of childhood holidays and family gatherings. We describe mums and dads, brothers and sisters, nephews and nieces. But, at the same time, we find ourselves completely happy and content here. My work is so rewarding. The total involvement with the people is wonderful. I have discovered that the act of giving oneself completely to others is hugely fulfilling and I couldn't ask for anything more, either spiritually or professionally. Indeed, I am incredibly lucky and really grateful. Communication becomes easier every day and my confidence increases with the problems that I face. My heart sometimes bubbles over with contentment and peace.

I am hoping to come home in November 1975. The other day I read: *"In all your ways acknowledge Him and He will direct your path."* I pray that God will show me what I must do with the rest of my life. I can only try to be a Christian servant wherever I may find myself. I pray every day for patience, kindness, gentleness, joy and peace, and trust that I will possess a few more of these good things by the time I come home.

Now it is Monday and it's 3.00 p.m. The front of my bungalow is looking more cultivated nowadays. The path to the gate divides the garden into mustard plants on the left, just bursting into brilliant yellow flowers, and *saag* (a very leafy and tasty version of spinach) on the right. The gardener is squatting in the middle of the foliage doing a spot of weeding. There is a cool breeze blowing through the trees on the other side of the lane and occasionally an ox cart, a bullock or a few goats pass the gate. I defeated everybody at gin rummy last night! It must have been all the practise we had on our childhood holidays in Ogmore.

My verses for today were from the prophet Habakkuk: *"Though the fig trees do not blossom, nor fruit be on the vines, the produce of the olive fail and the fields yield no food, the flock be cut off from the fold and there be no herd in the stalls, yet I will rejoice in the Lord, I will joy in the God of my salvation. The Lord is my strength; He makes my feet like hinds' feet; he makes me tread upon my high places.*" This seems to sum up perfectly the way the villagers think in this desperately poor part of the world. Despite their poverty, you often hear the phrase "*Ishwar Prem*" (God is love).

6 November Wednesday

We are here on the floor of the main room, sitting in the middle of a new consignment of drugs from *Dhaka*. We've had a good day at *Meherpur*, travelling there and back by Land Rover for the first time since the rains stopped. This means the journey takes an hour both ways rather than the three or four hours by boat. Florence and Lizzie are off to *Dhaka* tomorrow for some medical meetings, so there will just be two of us for the rest of the week. Meg and Pat are still in England travelling around the country, speaking about our work here.

12 November Tuesday

New Land Rover

I'm sitting here on the back veranda all alone, watching the ducks paddling up the river. On the far side there must be a wedding somewhere as I can hear singing and music coming from quite a long way away. Florence and Lizzie have just arrived back from *Dhaka* with a VSO called Rachel, who has come up-country for a change of scenery. They have brought a new Land Rover with them, donated by the Swiss churches for our family planning and community health work. They had quite a journey coming back, taking two days to drive a hundred miles, crossing seven rivers on those precarious bamboo ferries. They spent an uncomfortable night sleeping on the roadside where they were troubled by mosquitos. Lizzie drove all the way.

Plans will soon be underway for rehearsing the nurses' nativity play and making the Christmas pudding. The Diocesan Synod will be coming to *Rotnapur* at the beginning of December to elect a new Bishop. Please pray that the Diocese makes the right decision. Where all the visitors are going to stay poses a problem, but we know that Keith, Ruby and Vicky are going to stay with us, giving them a nice break from the city. You'll remember how they flew out with me last year when Keith started the post of Diocesan Administrator.

When I told a little nine-year-old boy that I was writing to "*amar ma*" (my mother) he told me to send you his "*nomoska*" (greetings) He has been in the ward for the last five weeks with a broken femur. When he arrived, we gave him a little book with pictures of trees and houses in it. Never having seen a book before, he didn't understand what the drawings meant until they were explained to him.

24 November Sunday

A Surprisingly Large Catchment Area

Another lovely sunny Sunday afternoon, more and more birds having returned every day, till the birdsong is now as deafening as it was in February. I was hoping to get two or three letters written this morning after communion, but the ward was quite busy with three admissions and I didn't finish at the hospital until lunchtime.

We are making a full-scale map of the surrounding area of Bollobhpur and plotting all the villages where our outpatients come from. It's great fun trying to identify them on an old British High Commission map. For instance, at last week's men's clinic, we had patients from thirty-seven different villages within a fifteen-mile radius! And it can take an ox cart several hours to get here. When one considers that on that particular day only about half the villages in the area were represented, one begins to get an idea of the density of the population.

I spent an hour on the map again after lunch, so now, with the church bell ringing for evensong, I'm eventually getting down to my letters. Today is 'Stir Up Sunday' (the Sunday before Advent) and we should be stirring up the Christmas pudding, but we will have to wait until Lizzie and Eryl go to Calcutta next week and bring back at least some of the ingredients.

The evenings and mornings are getting quite nippy, but I haven't needed to use my sweaters which are looking quite fresh after their monsoon hibernation. I was rather sad to see that the cockroaches had been living in my best jacket and had eaten some holes in the lining, but, like the sweaters, it is now being aired in the sunshine and all will be well.

This lunchtime, having seen ninety men singlehanded, I was invited, with the others, to lunch at the home of one of the nurses. It was very peaceful sitting on the veranda of her home with a large, thatched roof sheltering us from the hot sunshine. Each family compound is made up of mud houses, several generations living around a small central area. Eating, sleeping and the activities of day-to-day life take place on the veranda, the inner room being used for the storage of the few possessions that they have. Bengali families sleep altogether. They do not understand our Western custom of sleeping in different rooms and the idea of putting each child in a separate bedroom is considered strange, if not cruel.

The chickens and ducks were pecking around, and one or two cows were munching at some straw. The girls had been husking rice in the middle of the compound, so there was a large heap of husks which attracted the chickens before they were chased off by several little boys and girls. On this particular occasion, we were able to eat without being watched by twenty or thirty villagers. The rice meal was magnificent and we wobbled back to the hospital feeling full! Later on, when we were sitting on the back veranda, we could see clouds of smoke rising beyond the trees on the far side of the river and we heard lots of shouting and excitement. Fire spreads rapidly in the villages because of the thatched roofs. We heard later that no-one was injured although it was a nasty fire with two or three houses going up.

Lizzie has just come to call me to go with her to the Catholic Fathers at *Bobapar*, five miles away, for tea. We want to borrow some tomato plants from them. It's a funny climate: we can eat only what is in season and we haven't seen a tomato for eight months, but after Christmas there will be nothing *but* tomatoes for three months, huge, gorgeous ones. Lizzie says thank you very much for all the delicious packets of soup you send. They make the housekeeping job much easier.

Unfortunately the post is unreliable at the moment and we're lucky to get post once a week. But when the letters *do* come, it's lovely to hear all the news although it was sad to hear about the terrible bomb attacks in Birmingham. At the moment, England seems to be a more dangerous place to live in than over here. I'm glad I was in Dublin in the sixties and not the seventies.

More Work for the Vet
Tom and Di's dog had an accident six months ago and must have fractured her pelvis. She's been unable to deliver her first litter of pups these last few days so I was called in to help with the deliveries. Unfortunately the pups were born dead, but I think there's another one still to come. Of all the things I had anticipated before I arrived here, I hadn't expected to be a veterinary surgeon! Still, it's all good experience because the goat I delivered three months ago is doing fine.

Yesterday I removed a large ovarian cyst from a lady. It was about the size of a football, the operation lasted an hour and a half. I was feeling quite rough and thought I might have been getting a touch of flu, but I'm feeling fine again today. It's been a year since I arrived in Bollobhpur! What wonders I have seen, both medical and spiritual!

If anyone is wondering about sending me a gift for Christmas, just one Gillette razor blade in a letter would arrive safely and be happily received! I have a full beard at present because someone pinched the very last of my blades a month ago. Still, I expect they will make better use of them than I would.

Last night we ate baked beans for the first time in twelve months! What bliss! It's wonderful to find that many people are sending us packets of soup and donations for the work here. I'm taking a note of all the people that you mention in your letter and will write to them personally after Christmas. I am very thrilled to hear of everyone's concern and grateful for their kind gifts. We must thank God for this outpouring of love. The reason why He gives us so much help each day and why life and work here are so filled with satisfaction and joy must surely be the result of the prayers of so many people.

26 November Thursday

I find myself weighing 11st 10lb today. My weight has gradually dropped off because of the high carbohydrate/low fat diet. My Marks and Spencers cotton slacks have survived remarkably well. Having just two pairs of trousers makes life simple – I wear one pair on one day, whilst the other pair is being washed down at the river, and then the following day I swap them round.

Lizzie and Eryl are going to buy me two new Indian shirts in Calcutta tomorrow, so I should be looking very smart for Christmas. My traveller's cheques are still untouched, so don't worry about my needing any money. Your idea of asking your friends to send Christmas cards to the orphanage is lovely. I will address them to the individual boys and girls and let you know their names. Thank you so much for your kindness.

8 December Sunday

Florence, Lizzie, Eryl and I are sitting down in front of a log fire with an after-dinner cup of tea. It's quite cold in the evenings now and the fire is necessary. Unfortunately, the chimney isn't very effective and there's more smoke coming into the room than going up the chimney! But we can't have everything! We had a great meal of egg and bacon brought back from Calcutta by Lizzie and Eryl – absolutely super. They'd also bought some sausages, but somebody pinched them while they were waiting to cross the border!

After a night of worry, I did a caesarean section this morning and everything went well with Lizzie scrubbing and Eryl anaesthetising with the EMO machine. The girl's condition continues to be critical; her high blood pressure having been the reason for operating.

Bimal Mallick

As I was walking across to the hospital a couple of nights ago, I met a villager called *Bimal Mallick*. He was only wearing a thin vest and a ragged pair of shorts. I commented on his cold hands and he replied (in *Bangla* of course): *"When you're cold, give thanks to God, and when you are hungry give thanks to God, and when you are in obhab* (need) *give thanks to God,"* and here in the poorest country in the world, with a *million* stars above us, I shared an old man's prayer of thanksgiving the like of which I had never experienced before. It was a living testimony to those verses from Habakkuk that I quoted a few weeks ago: *"Though the fig tree does not blossom, nor fruit be on the vines … yet I will rejoice in the Lord, I will joy in the God of my salvation."*

13 December

Christmas is Coming

Things are getting quite Christmassy! We're practising the nurses' nativity play every evening at 6.00 p.m. My part of King Herod is coming along, but the *Bangla* is proving a little difficult to learn. The nurses seem to think it's alright and giggle like mad when I do my big angry speech at the end! I'm sure it'll be alright on the night.

I can hear carols coming from both church and a small open-sided thatched chapel where the nurses pray. Many of the tunes are ones that we know, such as *Hark the Herald Angels* and *O Come All Ye Faithful*. We're having our first quiet evening since the Diocesan Council descended on Tom at *Rotnapur* last week. Eighty delegates from all over Bangladesh arrived, staying for two days and then disappearing again. The transport problem was enormous since we are ten miles from the nearest road and *Rotnapur* is another three miles beyond us. But everything went off well and a new bishop has been elected. Keith, Ruby and Vicky stayed with us and thoroughly enjoyed the change.

Three days ago an engineer came from *Dhaka* to mend our X-ray machine. It seems to be working well again whenever electricity permits, so it will be extremely useful for broken bones and chests especially. There is such a lot of TB in this part of the world and it's good to be able to confirm the diagnosis quickly.

I'm fit and well and pleased to have managed to get a day off down at *Rotnapur* this week. Before he married Dianne, Tom spent several years with the Oxford Mission Fathers in *Barisal*. He tells some wonderful stories about the monks there: following the death of one old chap, it was discovered that he had kept in a notebook a record of every pudding he had eaten in the previous thirty years! Another old monk, who had failing eyesight, was reading out a passage from the Book of Job which describes the crocodile. The verse reads: "*His underparts are like sharp potsherds.*" In the poor light, he mistakenly read: "*His underpants are like sharp potsherds.*" The silent brothers were convulsed with laughter!

Tom has had an interesting life! Before his years in the monastery, he was a sailor in the Merchant Navy. He still smokes a lot of Burmese cheroots. Where he gets his supply from, I've no idea!

20 December

I'm writing to you as we sit on the front veranda in warm sunshine, all the more welcome because it's now so bitterly cold in the early morning and the evening. We wrap ourselves up in blankets until 10.30 a.m. each morning but even at lunchtime it's a bit nippy in the house. The afternoons are lovely, warm, and fresh, and it's nice to lie out on the grass after lunch for an hour or two.

Everyone is getting excited about Christmas. The nurses' nativity play is coming along well and we've been practising every night. As you can guess, I'm very much enjoying the part of King Herod and they think it's grand, especially the angry bits where my *Bangla* comes out with a strong Welsh accent! "*Who is this child who must be King of the Jews?*" Everyone is happy and the shepherds' scene is a real hoot, more dialogue being added every night. Today is the final rehearsal for the performance. I wish you could see it. I'm also accompanying the little children's nativity play in the church on Monday afternoon, when they sing Bengali carols to the tunes of *God Rest You Merry Gentlemen* and *Silent Night*.

27 December Sunday

Christmas Begins with a Surprise Message from London

This evening I'm writing by candlelight in front of the fire. After a wonderful and joyful Christmas, it is nice to have a little peace and quiet again. Where can I start to describe these last few days! We've all been inspired by the genuine joy and happiness of those around us – crowds of people, crowds of children, songs and dances.

We always try to listen to the service from St. Martins-in-the-Fields in London on the BBC World Service at 5.00 p.m. on a Sunday. Occasionally, the Reverend Austin Williams starts off the broadcast by sending greetings to special people across the world. Well, last Sunday, he sent greetings to "*Florence, Julian, Eryl and Lizzie in Bangladesh!*" We were very thrilled that Pat must have had a chat with him when she was in London.

On Christmas Eve our nativity play, performed at the far end of the ward, went off well. The costumes were created on the spot out of the nurses' beautiful saris and sewn on to the characters. The baby ward doubled as the 'wings'. Every time a baby cried someone picked it up to quieten it, so that, at one point, there were three Kings, a pair of shepherds and Herod all holding babies whilst waiting to go on.

Then we had dinner and, after having great fun putting up the decorations in the house (just a few balloons and one or two paper roses), we settled down and had coffee and mince pies to listen to the festival of carols from King's College crackling through the radio. Soon it was time to help the nurses decorate the hospital chapel. The night was clear and crisp, but it was chilly and we were glad to get back to the fire.

We went to midnight communion, wrapped up in blankets just like the villagers around us who were singing the Bengali carols and *Son Kerton's* with great gusto and rhythm. It was very moving in the flickering light of oil lamps and candles, especially *Glory to God in the Highest*. When communion was over at 1.30 a.m. there was just time to say Happy Christmas and to get into bed.

Christmas Day

At 5.00 a.m. the nurses arrived at the bungalow with Eryl and Lizzie. They stood on the veranda, dancing and singing and clapping their hands. I got dressed and joined them, firstly going to the orphanage and then back to the hospital chapel, where we sat on the reed mats and sang and sang. At about 6.00 a.m., as I was going back to bed to catch another hour's sleep, I passed the home of my nearest village neighbours. It was just light and they invited me to sit by the fire with their three little children, appropriately named Elizabeth, Gabriel and Mary, as they made special Christmas pies which they would eat later in the day.

A breakfast of fried egg and a tomato (the first tomato of the year) was followed by a ward round. The nurses giving out old Christmas cards and biscuits to the patients whilst telling them the story of Christmas. There were warm woollies for the babies and children. A little boy with a broken leg received an empty Sellotape reel on the end of a piece of string. What pleasure he got from it!

By now, the villagers were beginning to crowd into the church and much singing was going on. I gave out over thirty Christmas cards to the village children. Then all the nurses, orphans and staff came into the house to receive their Christmas presents. You can't imagine how much they appreciated them! They were thrilled. More people were pouring into the compound and there was great fun and laughter.

The Celebrations are Interrupted

In the middle of all this, a medical emergency arrived in a bullock cart: a ten-year-old boy had been stabbed in the night. Surgery would be necessary, so we said goodbye to the celebrations and got back into our working clothes. Within three quarters of an hour the lad was on the table and anaesthetised. As with all penetrating abdominal wounds, I had to find out whether there was any internal damage – but he was already shocked and in a bad state. After an hour and a half, I had found and sutured three holes in his intestine. I was beginning to come out again, suturing each layer one by one, grateful that we'd identified the damage and repaired it. *Then, quite suddenly, his heart stopped* and, despite all our resuscitative measures, there was nothing we could do to save him. We were speechless and quite taken by surprise although we knew that his condition was extremely poor even before we had started. The relatives heard the news outside and began to wail, the sound mingling with the carols of the crowds going into the church. What an incredibly sad thing to happen on Christmas morning, but we had done our absolute best.

The Day Moves On

In the afternoon, after a lunch of tinned ham, six or seven groups of *Son Kerton* singers stood on the front steps of the house with the villagers clapping and dancing. The music went on until well after dark, when the crowds had gone home and just the nurses and ourselves were left on the steps still singing *Silent Night* and *Come to my heart Lord Jesus* both in *Bangla* and English. Then Lizzie, Eryl, Florence, Bryan (from *Rotnapur*) and myself had a magnificent goose dinner by candlelight, followed by a 'poor man's' Christmas pudding, so called because any ingredient which isn't available is substituted by anything that comes to hand!

Despite the sadness of the morning, we were in good spirits, helped no doubt by a bottle of wine that had been left by our friends from *Dhaka*. After the meal, we sat in front of the fire and opened our presents. I received a book from Florence, an Indian shirt from Lizzie and Eryl and two razor blades from Bryan. I had given him five old blades of my own that I'd cleaned up and polished. I had given a toothbrush to Florence and a needle and cotton to Lizzie. What fun it is to give small gifts when everything is useful!

We sang along to the guitar and played Happy Families until we were beginning to drop off to sleep in front of the fire. We were in bed by 11.00 p.m. What a lovely Christmas to remember!

I must finish writing now, before the oil lamp dies down.

Chapter 3

1975

3 January

Letter to the Headmaster of Newport High School

May I convey our grateful thanks to the pupils of Newport High School. It is wonderful to read that the boys and girls should feel a connection between themselves in a very modern school and a little village of mud-built houses in the middle of Bangladesh where life has remained much the same for hundreds of years.

In my short time here at Bollobhpur, I have already learnt so much that it would be hard to put it all into words. But it isn't unknown that people like myself, who come to the poorer countries of the world presuming that they are going to teach, find that it is they themselves that are being taught, and others who come hoping to 'do good', discover that far greater good is being done to them. In this remote village hospital, ten miles from the nearest main road, with very few of the resources that we have come to rely upon in the West, there is a much stronger sense of God's presence. To quote St. Paul: *"Hard-pressed on every side we are never hemmed in; bewildered, we are never at our wits' end."* Our drug stocks dwindle to practically nothing before another supply appears; our operating light works intermittently, but its sporadic activity often coincides with major surgery; I operate under such limitations as would be considered unacceptable at home, yet I have witnessed extraordinary recoveries for which I cannot really account.

10 January Friday 3.00 p.m.

Grace Sufficient

Yesterday I performed an emergency tracheostomy on a nine-month-old baby girl who was struggling to breathe. It was the first such procedure that I had performed on an infant and we were all happy beyond words to see the relief that she immediately experienced from the frightful breathing difficulties which had brought her into the hospital. And what a coincidence that it happened this week of all weeks when Dad is undergoing his laryngectomy.

I am encouraged by 2 Corinthians 12 v.9 which records God's answer to Paul's repeated prayers for help: "*My grace is sufficient for you, for my power is made perfect in weakness.*" God's grace is not only adequate but freely available in times of need. We do not need to ask for it, because it has already been given and it only remains for us to accept.

26 January Sunday 9.00 a.m.

The Gearbox Lets Us Down

It's a fresh sunny Sunday morning and I'm looking out on the abundant flowers in my garden! Last weekend, I drove the big vehicle down to *Khulna* with Florence and thirteen children who were catching the steamer back to school in *Barisal*. I can't remember when I've experienced such a hazardous drive before, for in many places the road was only a little wider than the jeep with uneven hard shoulders on either side. Each mile south seemed to be crowded with bullock carts, water buffalo, bicycles, chickens, goats and overloaded country buses and, in every little village and town we drove through, groups of men were standing on the road talking to one another.

We were welcomed by the Anglican priest with whom I had stayed on my way up from language school a year ago, a wonderfully kind and hospitable man. Unfortunately, the gearbox packed up while we were there, so it was a good job that *Driver* had followed us in the other Land Rover with an extra half dozen children. A man of few words, he worked by torchlight, repairing it by Sunday morning. On our return journey we stopped at an impressive market, where everything was being sold, from vegetables to opium. We saw villagers using the joints of their fingers to count in units of four. We bought three chickens for Lizzie, who promises us eggs for breakfast every day but, since we returned to Bollobhpur, the chickens have so far not obliged! We arrived back just after dark and found that Lizzie and Eryl had been having rather an awful day with a difficult obstetric case. They were certainly relieved to see us.

On Thursday evening, a two-year-old girl came in with a very nasty gash on her forearm and it took me an hour or more to put in twenty-seven stitches. But she is progressing well and won't have a bad scar, I hope.

Lizzie has become proficient at suturing too, recently putting sixty stitches in a girl's leg. She has also learnt the technique of anaesthetic blocks and forceps deliveries. She's very practical.

Tunu's Wedding

Last Friday we all went off to *Tunu's* wedding in *Nitanandapur*, about eight miles the far side of *Meherpur*. She had been the senior nurse at Bollobhpur for twenty years and was highly respected. We arrived in time to see the bridegroom turning up in his bullock cart. The church was crowded and the service was short, but the vows were the same as at home. Then there was a great celebration to the accompaniment of a bagpipe band. I was persuaded to put on a colourful *sari* and dance in front of a hundred and fifty villagers, who cheered and clapped! A huge feast followed with marvellous curries served on banana leaves. There seemed to be hundreds of children everywhere, as excited and chatty as ever. It is sad to be losing *Tunu*, who is such a good nurse and has become a friend too. Her new husband is a male nurse and they are going to work in a hospital on the other side of Bangladesh, near *Chittagong*. She had only ever seen the bridegroom twice before the wedding and had never spoken to him, so she was naturally apprehensive!

We arrived back about 7.00 p.m. and enjoyed the packet of soup that you had sent us, sitting in front of a log fire. It is still very cold at both ends of the day and I have four blankets on my bed. However, it clouded over and rained in the middle of the week and immediately it was a little warmer. This has been the first rain since September and it was delightful to hear the sound of the downpour. We rushed out onto the veranda and just stood there and listened and looked! The following morning, as I walked across to the hospital, I enjoyed that unmistakable smell of the countryside. It reminded me of our walks along the cliffs from Ogmore to Southerndown as children, looking for mushrooms. At last the dust has settled and the garden has been freshened up by the rain.

Unkind Words

As we were preparing to return from *Meherpur* last week, a man asked us if we would transport his recently deceased father back to Bollobhpur in the Land Rover. As it was already full to capacity with ourselves, a new mum and her baby, boxes of drugs and medical equipment, we explained, rather impatiently, that it was not practical to do so. Some hours later, the late gentleman arrived in Bollobhpur strapped into a bicycle rickshaw. I felt very guilty that we had not been kinder.

Bengali Curries

Have I ever told you about the curries we eat nearly every day? They are mostly vegetable based – potato, spinach, ladies' fingers (okra) and there is always a good helping of *dhal*. There is a saying that, if you find the bay leaf in your portion, it means that you are going to receive a letter. About twice a week we have goat meat or fish. Occasionally we have *rui* fish which, I understand, is considered to be a bit of a delicacy. In the village, an honoured guest will receive the fish head, but we do not follow the custom ourselves!

28 January Tuesday 5.00 p.m.

Many thanks for your lovely parcel full of programmes, a handkerchief, note pads and a picture postcard of Wales. As you can imagine, I had great fun opening it and discovering what was inside.

I've just finished the baby clinic and enjoyed a cup of tea and a slice of bread and marmalade. We won't have any butter until Florence returns from *Dhaka*. Back in the house, I'm trying to write a letter or two before dinner. We've had a quiet week, by which I mean that there have been no major surgical or obstetric emergencies, although at the moment we have an unconscious diabetic patient. We can't help him because we have no insulin. The relatives hope to get hold of a supply in a town forty miles away, but they won't return until tomorrow afternoon at the earliest. I hope that the patient survives until then, but, sadly, I have little confidence that he will. Drugs are exceedingly difficult to obtain here in Bangladesh and we find our stocks are getting low again.

9 February Sunday 2.00 p.m.

A Houseful

Another clear and beautiful day with a gentle warm breeze making it all very refreshing. The birds are singing, just as they were almost a year ago when I sat in the garden and recorded my first message to you. The weather is perfect. We have been rather overwhelmed by visitors from *Dhaka,* who have come to stay for a few days, and a Finnish lady who is travelling around the country. The young people are really nice: two English chaps of my own age. One of them had been a Benedictine monk for six years and was interesting to talk to. "*I'm trying to see if God can do without me for a while,*" he said! There is also a Scottish girl and a Dutch girl, both volunteers.

We had twelve at dinner on Saturday night, followed by an evening singing round the fire, although these last few evenings have been almost too warm to merit one. It's very pleasant to have all these visitors, but Lizzie struggles to find enough food for us all. It is a real problem for her and she sleeps badly worrying about it.

We've been invited to a wedding feast in the village and we're waiting to be called. As one reads in the Bible stories, someone will come and say, "*The meal is now ready!*"

I am in the best of health, full of the joys of spring and no longer troubled by abscesses. Work is quiet at the moment, so I'm having a few days relaxing and reading. The hospital works efficiently and any emergency is dealt with very rapidly. I am making the most of this gorgeous weather. My garden is looking lovely with beans, peas, and flowers.

5.00 p.m.: I've just returned from the wedding feast, where we ate a huge pile of rice and vegetables served, as always, on banana leaves. We were nearly bursting! Lizzie will post this letter in Calcutta in a day or two. I am hoping to have three weeks' holidays in the second half of April, either in Nepal or *Kashmir* where they say the scenery is outstanding. I will bring this letter to an end now as the mosquitoes are beginning to bite my ankles.

11 February

Shrove Tuesday

We are sitting here after dinner, having just shared a bottle of wine which Florence brought back from *Dhaka* – a present from the Canadian High Commissioner! So please excuse my writing because my head is a little dizzy!

We had pancakes for our meal tonight – a nice change from *ruti* (flatbread) which we eat for breakfast every day. The latter are made from brown flour and oil, which we roll up to eat. Quite naturally, without thinking, we rolled our pancakes up and ate them with our fingers!

Tomorrow is Ash Wednesday, so we've been wondering what we should give up for Lent. After much discussion, we have decided to forgo bread, butter and jam for tea and have a silent breakfast every Wednesday. Experiencing a silent breakfast at the Oxford Mission was wonderful, where the only sounds to be heard were the grinding of ancient dentures and milk being poured over the cornflakes.

I've just been reading a book called *Enough Is Enough* by John Taylor, the new Bishop of Winchester. He writes about the Western world's excessive consumption of food and fuel, describing it as ruthless and unthinking. It is really a revelation and well worth reading. I am recovering from an abscess on my chest, but please don't be anxious as I've never been so well and happy.

17 February Monday

Beethoven after a Sad Day

Eryl, Lizzie and I are listening to a tape recording of Beethoven's *Pathétique Sonata* in front of the fire – absolutely beautiful. It is very calming and pleasant after a traumatic day.

A *poate* was admitted in labour, haemorrhaging badly. I was doing the clinic, but the girls got everything ready for a caesarean section in record time. We had to wait for Eryl to come back from *Meherpur* to give the anaesthetic. She arrived an hour and a half later than had been expected and, by that time, I was on tenterhooks. Anyway, the caesarean section went perfectly. Everyone was efficient to a degree and I completed the caesar in less than forty minutes, which was a record. Our joy was short-lived, however. The girl had been so desperately unwell beforehand and her blood pressure fell further an hour later. She did not improve and died soon after, despite all our efforts. If only we had blood. What a sad end to the day, but we felt that we had done our utmost. We have such critically ill obstetric patients here, far worse than any obstetrician at home could ever imagine. However, it's amazing how many of them do well and go home. Only recently, I saw two of my 'caesar' ladies with healthy six-month-old babies and that cheered me up no end.

I've mentioned before how so many of these operations are undertaken with insufficient light, the generator working only intermittently. That leaves us with making use of reflected sunlight in the daytime and handheld battery torches when it is dark.

Another woman died from tetanus (lockjaw) today, a very distressing end for anyone. She'd had ten children and probably developed tetanus in her efforts to terminate a further pregnancy. But I mustn't depress you with all this. Last Thursday I performed an appendicectomy on an extremely ill chap and he's doing remarkably well. I myself have fully recovered from my chest abscess. It was drained and I had many good nurses looking after me. Once again I'm as fit as a fiddle, very happy and full of gratitude to God for all His goodness to me.

I am so pleased to hear of Dad's remarkable progress following his laryngectomy. Please give him my love and encouragement. I am sure that he has recovered so quickly as a result of many prayers.

Coping with Bitterness

I believe that nothing can destroy us. Nothing that we do (or have done) can separate us from God's love. I also believe that God can change our personalities, and those things that are impossible *without* Him become possible *with* Him. He is changing my personality – I know it because I so often ask for the Fruits of the Spirit – gentleness, patience, love, joy and compassion. He helps us to forgive others when we feel that we cannot forgive. He who can turn sadness into joy and weakness into strength can surely turn our bitterness into forgiveness and understanding. We must start off believing that He *can* do it and persist in our prayers, confident that He *will* do it.

When Jesus said, *"love your enemies and pray for your persecutors,"* we were being told to love and pray for them even though they haven't asked for our forgiveness and have no intention of doing so. For through forgiving we are forgiven.

How wonderful to hear that Newport High School has sent another £50. I intend to write and thank them again. Gosh, I hear that petrol has gone up to 75p a gallon! I'm wondering if I'll be able to afford a car when I return. Thank you so much for the magnificent packets of soups, which you kindly send and are much appreciated by all, and, of course, the occasional *South Wales Argus* which is read from cover to cover by everyone.

Tuesday

A message came through from *Meherpur* about an obstetric lady who was in difficulties so we jumped in the jeep and drove over there. Not exactly the 'Flying Squad' though, because the road is in such a bad condition and we were delayed at the bamboo ferry at *Krishnagar*. We scarcely managed fifteen miles an hour on the way there. Four hours later, when we brought the lady back, her drip swinging from the roof, we could only manage five miles per hour, *Driver* desperately trying to avoid the bumps and the potholes. The lady is well and recovering satisfactorily today. Again, I tried to record a tape this afternoon, but another *poate* was admitted in obstructed labour, so the afternoon was practically gone.

Wednesday 8.30 a.m.

Two Caesars
I'm sitting here in *Meherpur* at the beginning of our clinic. We arrived early this morning with the intention of getting ahead of the crowds, which, of course, is how we like it. There will be a steady flow until 1.00 p.m. The morning is far more manageable when we get here early. It's much better than trying to cope with a hundred men all fighting to get into my consulting room at the same time with an equal number of women doing the same thing at the other end of the building.

We've had quite a busy twenty-four hours, having ended up doing a caesarean section yesterday evening (mother doing well). Now, after a busy clinic here in *Meherpur*, we will go straight back after lunch to do yet another caesarean. We've left Lizzie at Boll. to sort things out after yesterday's surgery and prepare for this afternoon's operation!

In the meantime, three people have come from the Christian Healthcare Project in *Dhaka* which, at present, is our only source of drugs. The group includes a girl who has been to Bollobhpur before and two Swedes, a young man and his wife. So, just at the moment, we don't have much time to ourselves.

Pat came back from the UK last Saturday, and Lizzie and I went to meet her at the Indian border sixty miles away. It was quite a tiring drive but a pleasant change from the hospital work. Pat was well and rested. She has put on a stone in weight! She brought a lot of things back with her including numerous packets of food, much to our delight. The Dream Topping which you sent a few weeks ago was put on top of the birthday cake which Lizzie had baked for Eryl.

24 February Monday 3.30 p.m.

Village Dogs

A lot of mangy looking dogs hang around the village and don't seem to belong to anyone. They are called pariah dogs or *pye-dogs*. They lurk around the hospital, scrounging for anything that they can steal or eat and we try to scare them away. As I was completing the surgery on that poor chap last year, one of these awful animals ran off with his amputated foot! Some of them belong to households and can be trained I understand, but the undomesticated ones are treated badly. I saw a half-starved dog tied to a post a few days ago and a group of kids were taking pleasure in stoning it.

The Ferry Nearly Capsizes

It's been quite a week in the operating theatre with two caesars, five tubal ligations and several finger amputations on top of the normal hectic life of outpatients and the ward rounds. On Wednesday, having manoeuvred the Land Rover onto the ferry (which, you will remember, is a bamboo platform stretched across two boats) it half capsized, nearly taking the vehicle and three mothers and their babies with it! Thankfully, I was able to reverse backwards off the ferry before any trouble. The river is only three feet deep now, so no harm was done and we all had a good laugh. After the momentary scare we got back to Bollobhpur, dry and in time to do another caesar.

It's good to hear of Dad's progress, but I'm sad to hear that he can't whistle any longer.

Introducing Father *Sushil*

An exciting month lies ahead: Father *Sushil* is coming from the Oxford Mission in Calcutta to conduct a retreat from March 3rd to the 8th. He is much loved by all. On some of the days he will address the nurses in Bengali and, on others, he will give talks to us in English. He's a dear old man who, years ago, walked sixty miles to give communion to a dying lady. Nowadays, he is very overweight, wears a white cassock and travels around the country on a motorbike. He recalls how as a young Hindu he witnessed the burning of some Christian books. He picked up a piece of charred paper on which was printed, "*I am the light of the world.*" This led to his conversion and a lifelong ministry. I'm not certain when he became a monk.

Immediately after his departure the Eye Camp will begin when three government surgeons arrive and hopefully perform a hundred cataract operations in two days. This will require a great deal of organisation on our part simply coping with the extra patients. It's been quite a sight already seeing many old chaps with long beards coming in from all over the district to register for the surgery and bringing their wives too. The news is spreading quickly. It will be an extremely busy time and I don't know where we are going to put all the patients. It'll be joyful chaos, I expect, and we are very much looking forward to it.

The British Consul visited us recently. I understand he makes sporadic visits to ex-patriots out in the wilds. He brought a bottle of gin with him and I had my first taste of gin and tonic. It may have established a lifelong habit!

Holiday Plans

I have finally settled plans to spend three weeks in Nepal at the end of April with Bryan, the VSO based at *Rotnapur*. It should be quite a holiday. We're hoping to do some trekking in the Himalayas, but it all depends on passports and visas.

Time is passing so quickly and everything is wonderful. The birds are fascinating, even more so since we have acquired a new pair of field glasses. We spend a lot of our time identifying them: many kinds of kingfishers, bee-eaters, bulbuls, hoopoes (with their colourful crests) and brain-fever birds. The call of the brain-fever bird ascends the scale until it nearly drives you mad and then it starts at the bottom again! It's just like a bird sanctuary here. The wildlife too is fascinating. We recently saw a three-foot lizard stalking his way through the garden and occasionally we spot a porcupine. Everything is oversized here: the ants and bees are massive compared to home. The skies are blue and the weather today is cool and refreshing.

27 February

Cucumbers and Communion Wine
Yesterday we got back from *Meherpur* just after dark at 7.30 p.m. and had a cold meat salad with cucumbers, which are in season at the moment. Unfortunately, because of the dimness of the lamps, Eryl mistook the bottle of *communion wine* for the bottle of *vinegar.* It got poured over the cucumber and, after a few mouthfuls, just when I was about to comment that the vinegar had 'gone off', it began to dawn on us what had happened and we all roared with laughter.

The lady, whom we had brought back from *Meherpur* yesterday, is well and recovering satisfactorily today. Another *poati* was admitted in obstructed labour this afternoon and occupied much of the afternoon. It's now 5.00 p.m.

Exotic Tastes
A senior member of the Diocese was with us last weekend. I was impressed by his willingness to conform to our strange Western breakfast customs – at breakfast, I noticed he applied both marmite *and* marmalade to his *ruti*, the one carefully layered on top of the other, and appeared to enjoy it.

3 March Monday 3.15 p.m.

The Retreat Begins

I am writing to you early, as tomorrow dear old Father *Sushil* will lead our retreat. He is sitting in the room next to me right now with his feet up. The retreat began this morning in the hospital chapel with a communion for the nurses, half of whom will be silent today. This has left the wards almost empty of staff, so Lizzie has had a great time bathing the babies and Pat's been quite frantic with a duster all morning. Thankfully, all is quiet.

The weather is getting steadily warmer again, though not sticky yet. I've removed the blankets from my bed and I'm back to writing letters in my swimming trunks. The prospect of a holiday in the mountains of Nepal couldn't be more appealing. Increasing numbers of blind people have been turning up to register for the Eye Camp next week.

Wednesday

Unfortunately, the Quiet Day wasn't as quiet as I had anticipated! I had a worrying delivery on my hands which kept me pacing up and down throughout the day and I only participated in the chapel services and addresses when I could. The outcome was that the mother was fine, but the baby died. Sad indeed, but it was a relief to us that the mother had survived.

Blind people from many surrounding villages have been coming up to register for the Eye Camp next week. The number of potential cataract candidates reached eighty-nine yesterday and it should be well over a hundred by the time the surgeon starts operating on Tuesday morning. It looks like we're going to have quite a few busy days ahead.

I noted that the local blind beggar of the village was not among those who had registered. Presumably he did not want to change his lifestyle. It is interesting that when Jesus passed the blind man, Bartimaeus, on the road to Jericho he asked him, "*What do you want me to do?*" although the beggar had shouted his head off to get some attention. Rather like the incident when he asked another sick person, "*Do you want to be healed?*" It would seem that some people don't want to be healed – they're happy with the way things are. I remember a sermon I heard from St Martin's-in-the-Fields on the radio last year, the Rector preaching on two words from the Bartimaeus story, "*Jesus stopped.*"

The birds are singing madly and my garden is producing a good crop of lettuces and lemons and the air is still and damp. I wonder what the weather is like at home. How is everyone reacting to the sudden rise in prices and the prospect of a new government? Unfortunately, all the radio sets are broken, so we don't hear the news very often.

The Touching of Feet and a Duck for Supper

We occasionally receive the greatest token of respect – the touching of our feet. I understand it is the ancient Hindu custom (adopted by Christians) of touching the feet of elders; for in doing so, one is blessed with wisdom and strength. One day when, in jest, I bent down to touch the nurses' feet, they recoiled and appeared perplexed.

We suddenly found ourselves longing for a taste of duck. *Mogul*, the cook, duly identified a suitable candidate in the village and, for a week, he was tied with a bit of string round his leg to a post outside the kitchen. When the great evening arrived we expectantly sat around the table waiting for the feast to arrive. Our faces dropped – one small, undernourished duck was certainly not going to go far among the five of us!

16 March Sunday

The Eye Camp

Last week we had the Eye Camp and what a wonderful experience it was! We took all the beds down and every square yard of floor and grass was covered with recumbent patients. The team of two doctors and two paramedics arrived on Monday and they were happy to discover that everything had already been organised. The professor arrived at midday the following day, a wonderful surgeon and a most humble gentleman. What a coincidence that he obtained his Fellowship at my old college in Dublin, so we had a lot to talk about. After a quick lunch he started to operate and worked solidly from midday until 9.00 p.m., except for a half-hour tea-break. He removed fifty cataracts, each one with the greatest care and precision. It was a pleasure to watch him. We had three operating tables in our small theatre with all of us coordinating the patients coming and going on stretchers, receiving their local anaesthetic blocks, holding torches and generally organising the smooth running of the ops. *Joton,* our watercarrier, functioned as a stretcher bearer and Bryan from *Rotnapur* had rigged up a car battery to give overall light. All those dear patients were so brave and so courageous with no panic or fuss, having had painful anaesthetic blocks around the eye, lying on the table, waiting for their turn with their hearts thumping, yet quite still, with their hands crossed or down by their sides. I haven't been so moved since I arrived in Bangladesh. By 9.00 p.m everyone was exhausted, Lizzie finally sweeping up the old cataracts from the floor with a broom.

After dinner we went to bed early, the professor hoping for a good night's sleep so that he would be ready for a further thirty operations the next morning. As soon as they had operated on the last patient, he and his assistants got into their jeep to drive to *Jessore* and fly back to *Dhaka*. It was a sad farewell, as we waved them off. All of us were nearly in tears: ourselves so impressed with the skills of the eye surgeon and the visiting team moved by the spirit of joy that pervaded our remote mission hospital.

And so I was left to manage eighty post-cataract patients! The following days were busy with large rounds every morning, checking each eye and instilling the correct drops. After the first week, only six patients are left. You can just imagine the happy bustle of that week! Toilet parades, food rounds and dressing rounds, with many patients still lying on the floor. There was special care for an old gentleman who got very confused the first night after his op. Now it's all over with just four patients on the mend and the miracle is that I didn't have one obstetric emergency the whole week. The Lord is good indeed!

19 March

Hard Work Takes Its Toll

It's now Wednesday at 9.00 p.m. and I'm writing after a particularly heavy day at the Meherpur Clinic. I've just admitted a four-month-old baby who has an incarcerated hernia. I'm afraid there's nothing much I can do for the infant with my limited experience in paediatric surgery, except hope that it will reduce spontaneously. Now a twelve-year-old boy has been admitted with an overdose.

Yesterday, Florence was shocked to discover that a thousand *taka* had been stolen from her room. The chief suspect was *Joton,* the watercarrier. Despite many protests of innocence, he was dismissed after much heart-searching by ourselves as to how to deal with the incident. We all got together to pray last evening, after the distress of the day, especially remembering Florence who is leaving soon and Pat who is taking over the heavy responsibility of the hospital. It was a lovely time of quiet.

To tell the truth, I have been getting progressively weary since the Eye Camp and rather reluctant to do anything routine such as read or write letters. Just in need of a change and a rest, I suppose, which I can soon look forward to. When you add it up, I've really only had one or two days away from work in six months.

Arriving back at 8.00 p.m. from *Meherpur* this evening, I had to do another obstetric procedure. Being on duty all the time (though not perhaps actually busy all the time) with ward rounds every morning, huge clinics, teeth to extract, fractures to reduce, complicated obstetrics and ops. of all kinds, it's a bit wearying, I suppose. But please don't worry, although I feel tired, no-one could be more fulfilled in their work and I am sure I will be fine after a break.

29 March Easter Saturday

Yesterday was Good Friday. We went to the church and sat through a service, with lengthy addresses delivered in *Bangla* by the village priest. It was a long three hours! Later on, Pat played a tape of Stainer's *Crucifixion*, which I've sung in Saint John's so many times since my childhood. We sat on the veranda eating hot-cross buns and listening to the beautiful music. In my last letter, I may have sounded a bit weary, but, as you can guess, after a pleasant and peaceful Good Friday, I have quickly found myself able to cope again and ready to go.

Our eye patients have done wonderfully well and a lot of them still come up for their daily drops. They are dear old souls. They'll receive their glasses in two weeks' time. The majority of them have done very well, with no signs of infection or other problems. Out of the eighty cataract operations performed in twenty-four hours, we had, in fact, only five complications – two haemorrhages, two infections and an iris prolapse. That so many of these good people have progressed so well since their surgery is yet another miracle. As usual, I've had the opportunity to learn more about eye surgery than I ever knew before. A good job too because yesterday I had to remove a half inch splinter of bamboo which had penetrated deeply into a four-year-old's eye.

Florence's Farewell

This last fortnight we have been doing the rounds of Florence's farewell in three of the local villages, with feasts and speeches, singing and dances, sweets and tea wherever we went. She is much loved in the area, having been at Bollobhpur for twenty-eight years. Everyone is deeply sorry that she is retiring since many of the villagers who were delivered by her now have hordes of children of their own. Last night we enjoyed a special send-off meal for her, and this morning, when she departed at 6.45 a.m. en route to *Jessore* airport, a great crowd of weeping nurses and villagers were on the veranda singing farewell songs and loading her with flowers.

Four minutes after the Land Rover had left the hospital compound we discovered that she'd forgotten her suitcase! Lizzie leapt into the other Land Rover with the intention of following her, but it wouldn't start. So I jumped on the nearest bicycle and pedalled as fast as I could down to *Rotnapur* to borrow the diesel jeep, scaring goats and scattering early travellers on the road. I brought the jeep back here, where Lizzie took over and drove like the clappers to catch them up, running over a chicken on the way. She went all the way to the airport before she caught sight of them, arriving only ten minutes before the flight was due to leave for *Dhaka*. Florence and *Driver* had discovered the absence of the case only five miles from Bollobhpur and were, of course, quite frantic wondering what to do.

2 April

Many thanks for the paperback which arrived on Easter Monday which I'm looking forward to reading. We read a lot, there being few other forms of entertainment here. Whenever anyone goes to Calcutta, we ask them to bring back a book from the Oxford Book Store in Park Street. "*Any book!*" we say. This means we have a regular supply of classics to read. At the moment I'm reading *Wuthering Heights*. Last month, I had many hours of pleasure from Thackeray's *Vanity Fair*. On the other hand, *Little Dorrit* by Charles Dickens, was slow-going and a little depressing.

Bandits

At the moment, *dacoits* (armed bandits) are terrorising the villages in the area and seldom a night goes by without someone having their life savings stolen. Fortunately, they haven't yet come to the hospital, but no-one can sleep peacefully. As my bungalow is several hundred yards from the hospital and I sleep alone here, I have been lying awake, wondering how I would react were they to come. It is very scary because there is no defence, no police and no security. We are so aware of the moonless nights of the month when it is literally pitch-black outside. Concern is widespread. Please pray for us that we may have courage to cope with the crisis and that these desperate men may turn their activities to the good of Bangladesh and not to its destruction.

6 April Sunday

Thunder Bolt

There was a tremendous thunderstorm yesterday. It was after lunch and we were sitting in the big room. You could hear the thunder approaching from miles away, until it sounded as if it were right overhead. Suddenly, there was a deafening thunderclap and a horizontal bolt of lightning shot through the house from the front terrace to the back, straight across the room where we were sitting. It was all over in a moment, but, as you can imagine, we were very shaken. They say that hundreds of people in Bangladesh are killed by lightning every year.

Progress with the Language

My Bengali is now reasonably fluent and I find it very strange that, not having spoken a foreign language before, I find myself *thinking* in Bengali without much effort. It is sometimes quite difficult to understand what the villagers are saying because of the local accent but we seem to understand one another quite well around the hospital and, on the few occasions that I leave the village, I can communicate quite well.

Lizzie and Eryl speak good Bengali too. They were on a train journey last year, sitting opposite a group of giggling ladies who didn't realize that the girls could understand their Bengali conversation. Confused by Lizzie's short hair, tunic top and trousers, one asked the other, "*Is it a man or a woman?*"

On another occasion, when Lizzie had struck up a conversation with a couple of fellow travellers, one of them was bold enough to ask, in Bengali, whether they were her own teeth and, when Lizzie replied in the affirmative, the lady responded in admiration: "*Khub sundor!*" ("Very beautiful!"). We've discovered that people here never like showing their teeth in photographs, that's why so many of them appear solemn.

There are two old villagers who turn up at the outpatients from time to time. I have taken to calling one of them '*Mr Nicely*' because that seems to be the only English word he knows. He is very polite and deferentially rubs his hands together, conveying his thanks by using the words "*Nicely, nicely*" over and over again.

The other gentleman, who makes an occasional visit to the clinic, uses a mixture of English and *Bangla* to express his frustration at the way the world is going: "*Eckibari gone to the dogs hoi gieche!*" he exclaims, which means "*Everything's gone to the dogs!*"

I went down to *Rotnapur* on Thursday to help deliver an obstructed cow. Fortunately, I arrived too late and the newborn calf was tentatively wobbling on its spindly little legs!

It's been getting hot and sticky over the last few days and I wear few clothes inside my house where nobody can see me. It's very dusty and we're looking forward to more of the April storms which were so pleasant this time last year, but not perhaps quite as dramatic as yesterday's thunder and lightning. I remember that, after each storm, the humidity dropped and it was quite cool and refreshing for a few days. At home, the countryside must be looking super. "*Oh, to be in England now that April's there!*" In my mind, I'm picturing the view from Llanhennock looking down on the Usk valley.

The insect life continues to impress me. Brilliantly coloured butterflies the size of the palm of your hand, wasps at least two inches long, great cockroaches and dragonflies too, all busy in the hot sunshine.

A Heap of Spectacles

The post-cataract patients returned today to receive their one-size-fits-all, regulation black framed glasses with thick lenses. I will never forget the joy and excitement expressed by everyone, regardless of their faith: Christians, Muslims and Hindus, all crowding into the nurses' chapel to give thanks that they were now able to see again after years of blindness. No greater shout of gratitude was ever heard!

A week tomorrow I will set off on holiday with Bryan and we are both looking forward to quite an adventure. Here's my itinerary: April the 13th to Calcutta, then a flight to *Kathmandu* on the 15th where we will stay until the 18th. From the city, a day-long bus journey will take us through the mountains of Nepal to *Pokhara* where we will stay with Bryan's missionary-doctor friend at the 'Shining Hospital'. After that we will spend a week trekking around the Annapurna Sanctuary. Having had only two or three days off-duty in six months, I'm not feeling in the best physical condition for twenty-miles-a-day walking, but I'm hoping that the mountain air will revive me. We hope to catch a view of the whole Himalayan range before we leave *Kathmandu*. Then back to the Indian border by bus to stay at another mission hospital at *Roxaul*, before travelling down to Calcutta by train. We're hoping to be back at Bollobhpur on Wednesday the 7th.

I must stop writing now, as I need to throw another bucket of water over myself. I'm very uncomfortable.

12 April Sunday 3.00 p.m.

Just a brief note to say that this afternoon I packed a rucksack with a sleeping bag, mosquito net and clothes for our holiday. We're hoping to leave at 6.00 a.m. tomorrow for the Indian border. I am really looking forward to it. I'm hoping that the fresh cool air of the Himalayas will put new life into me. Over the next few weeks, no doubt, there will be time for sitting around and reading or just looking at the mountains. How lucky we are! I can't wait for a steak in Calcutta because it will be the first one in a year!

Monday

Wellington Square, Calcutta
I thought I'd make the most of this opportunity of sending you a letter since we've met a couple of people from Yeovil who are travelling back to England on Friday and will take it with them.

Here we are in the middle of noisy, filthy Calcutta. Oh, such poor and ragged people! Innumerable people live on the streets, sleeping in shacks constructed of any material available, with piles of rubbish everywhere. Beggars, mostly maimed and old, sit on the pavements, and children and mothers with their babies follow us around for hours. Yet, despite all the misery, there seems to be a pervading sense of 'industriousness': the shoe-shine boys smile; the *wallahs* pull their rickshaws with energy and enthusiasm; everyone is active and busy.

We had our first glass of beer in nine months and a meal in a restaurant, but I was rather put off when a rat ran over my foot as I was eating it. Afterwards we went to the pictures, the film being rather ambitiously entitled *The Bible*! Films are hugely popular here in India and the cinema was crowded. We met some girls and arranged to meet them in *Kathmandu* at 7.00 p.m. outside the 'Green Hotel' a few days later. Their intention, unlike our own, was to travel up to Nepal by train. We are so looking forward to the mountains and cloudless skies of Nepal, hoping that the air will be more refreshing and invigorating than it is down here in Calcutta where it must be over ninety. I'll write again soon. I do hope all is well at home.

21 April Monday

Kathmandu

We flew north from Calcutta on the 15th and, not more than an hour later, we caught a glimpse of the Himalayan peaks. Our excitement grew as the plane made its final cautious approach into *Kathmandu* airport, cautious, that is, because the city is surrounded by mountains. Stepping off the plane onto the tarmac, we were mobbed by young Nepalese men promoting various hotels and we soon found ourselves in a sparsely furnished room in the heart of the old city. Later in the afternoon, we started to smarten ourselves up, ready to meet the girls that we had met in Calcutta. Arriving outside the agreed hotel at 7.00 p.m. we awaited their arrival but after half an hour there was still no sign of them. Feeling deflated we retreated to the nearest eating place, agreeing that, most probably, it would be the first and last time ever that we would be 'stood up' outside the 'Green Hotel' in *Kathmandu*!

What a fascinating place! It's just like stepping back four hundred years, with tiny streets flanked by stone houses, nearly touching one another, with beautiful carved wooden balconies overlooking the street. The city is full of squares of assorted sizes, little ones where the streets meet, and other big, paved ones with pagodas and temples on each side, adorned with exquisite statues and columns. All quite stunning. The streets are filled with shops selling vegetables and flowers, with traders hustling and bustling, and Buddhist monks, robed in brown and yellow, mingling with the crowd. The colours are particularly striking: red tomatoes, green onions, flowers of every variety and brightly patterned costumes. The people are happy, smiling and trying to make you laugh. We see attractive children everywhere, many of whom speak English. There are very few beggars here, or kids asking for *buckshees* and this comes as a real break from Calcutta and Bangladesh where the demand for handouts is persistent. There are lots of hippies and weirdly dressed Europeans and Americans here, but they seem to fade into the background of the city itself and do not spoil its ambience in any way. Tomorrow, we have an eight-hour bus drive westwards through the mountains to *Pokhara*. I feel so incredibly lucky to be here. It's unlikely that I'll see a post box for a week or two, but will write again as soon as I can, trusting that all is well at home.

3 May

'Shining Hospital', *Pokhara*

I hope you received my letter written in *Kathmandu* about nine days ago, describing the fascinating city and the friendliness of its people. After a hair-raising bus ride, swinging round precipitous corners and driving through awe-inspiring valleys, we arrived in *Pokhara* and made our way to the 'Shining Hospital', so called because of the sun's reflection on its tin roof.

We are guests of Bryan's friends, David and Beryl, who work as doctors in this little Nepalese Hospital. They and their three little children are most hospitable and kind, and soon after our arrival we were feeling very much at home. It was cloudy and raining on the day we arrived and there was little to see. But, just when we were wondering whether these legendary snow-capped Himalayan peaks were there at all, the clouds suddenly dispersed and, towering above us, silent and beautiful, stunningly white, almost ghostly, was the whole *Annapurna* range, with '*Machapuchare*' (which means 'Fishtail') rising to 24,000 feet, the sixth highest mountain in the world, only sixteen miles away from where we stood!

The *Annapurnas* filled the northern horizon, rising above forest-covered foothills, their pinnacles sometimes disappearing behind the clouds and then reappearing again as if by magic. I got up at 5.30 a.m. to see the dawn. It was awesome! At first, a tiny area of pink and gold struck the peaks, and slowly the whole range lit up. As the sun rose higher, the mountains changed into the purest snow-white and a new Nepalese day had dawned.

On Sunday morning, the family took us to their church, a little congregation of Nepalese Christians meeting together in a small building here in the foothills of the Himalayas – how amazing!

A few days later we set off to walk up through hillsides covered with wild rhododendrons and bamboo forests, across green-clad ridges, through valleys with cliffs towering above us, and alongside crystal mountain streams, foaming rivers and peaceful lakes. We passed lines of mules moving up and down the mountain passes, with bells around their necks and red plumes on their heads. We were greeted by single villagers winding their way along the paths with large wicker baskets on their backs, secured by a single strap across their foreheads. The baskets contained everything from chickens to household utensils and rice. We even saw a tiny little old lady being carried down the mountain in this way. What a way to carry your grandmother! We joined groups of chattering soldiers making their way up to the Chinese border and fellow travellers of all nationalities. Our general direction was always upwards, sometimes agonisingly so. On several occasions we ascended fifteen hundred steps cut into the mountainside and, having reached the ridge, straightaway descended an equal number of steps down into the next valley, only to be faced with another long climb on the opposite side. We passed through little Nepalese villages, staying in a lodge each night, eating rice and *dhal* with the locals and then bedding down on the floor. Each day we were overawed by the breathtaking scenery, with mountains peaks on each side and deep gorges falling away into the distance below us.

Mountain Rescue

One late afternoon, we arrived at *Ghorepani* at 10,100 feet, where we stayed in a little mountain hut, heated by a log fire constantly burning in the middle of the room and lit after dark by small oil lamps. A dozen trekkers sat around the fire, having shared what food they had; a few were smoking marijuana. Suddenly, an American burst through the door with the distressing news that his friend had fallen two hundred feet and was caught up in bushes and branches half a mile further up the mountain. We made a quick start with blankets, ropes and flaming torches. What a rescue team! Nepalese villagers, trekkers and even the lodge keeper, all of us excited and anxious, shouting guidance and instructions to each other in half a dozen languages! We found him unconscious, but not appearing to have fractured any bones, we strapped him on a make-shift stretcher and descended in the darkness, stumbling over rocks and bushes, the way lit only by the flaming torches. After three hours, he was back in the warmth of the lodge where he remained unconscious throughout the night with myself lying beside him on the floor, checking his observations, as best I could, by the flickering light of the fire and the waning oil lamps. The chap was still unconscious in the morning and a decision was made to send a runner down to *Pokhara,* from where a telegram could be sent to *Kathmandu* requesting a helicopter for his safe removal.

Lost on the Side of a Mountain

A day or two later, with three other trekkers, we left the hut to navigate our way across the mountain through thick forests to the next village on our journey. At 10,000 feet, we were still well below the snow line. This stage of the trek was known to be a difficult one because the tracks are renowned for leading off in wrong directions and sometimes disappearing altogether. We walked for nine and a half hours through dense woodland, often frustrated by false trails and dead-end tracks, and yet the occasional glimpses of snow-covered ridges above us were quite the most beautiful sights to be seen.

Finally it was getting dark. Exhausted and weary and not having a clue precisely where we were in fifty square miles of forest, we camped in a clearing and built a log fire to keep us warm through the oncoming night. The sky was crystal-clear and filled with a million stars and the fire burned for hours. We shared hot tea and ate some of the tinned stew that we had brought with us. In the grey light of the early morning, we noticed a little boy running through the trees and decided to follow his direction. To our relief, we discovered that we were only an hour away from the village which had been our original destination. Two days later, after many more adventures, we arrived back in *Pokhara* to a soft bed, a huge meal of eggs and bacon and a good rest. Although we nursed huge blisters and aching legs, we were overwhelmed by the beautiful scenery of Nepal – the experiences of the previous week being quite beyond my limited gifts of description.

13 May Twilight

Return to Bollobhpur

I'm sitting on the veranda at Bollobhpur at the end of a most refreshing and pleasant storm, the rain is now pouring off the roof gutters and dripping off the trees. The sparrows are beginning to sing again even though the thunder is still rumbling in the distance. I wrote my last letter from *Pokhara* about ten days ago, so I will quickly bring you up to date on a remarkable holiday.

A few days later we travelled back through the mountains to *Kathmandu*, and from thence, south to *Roxaul* on the Indian border. After several long train journeys and a night bedded down on a station platform with the locals and woken up early by country people bringing their vegetables in from the surrounding villages, we finally arrived back in Calcutta, where the temperature was 108! Later in the week we caught an early train north to the border where we were met by the ever-faithful *Driver*, who had been waiting for us with the Land Rover. Having performed a D&C on my way through *Meherpur*, we arrived back at Boll. about 4.30 p.m., where we received a great welcome.

Armed Police Arrive in the Village

The disturbing news when we got back was that a very frightening incident had occurred in our absence. One night Pat had been woken up and forced, at gunpoint, to admit a young political leader who had sustained five gunshot wounds. Everyone was sworn to secrecy with a threat of harm should the news become public. The wounds were already three days old and the man's condition was critical, requiring transfer to a bigger hospital. After a night of discussion and prayer, it was decided that *Driver* should take the patient to *Dhaka* in the four-wheel drive.

A day or two later, the police turned up asking if such a man had been admitted, and the girls were forced to tell them what had happened. Lizzie says that the whole incident was very scary, made even worse a few days later when two lorry loads of armed policemen turned up, establishing themselves in the village school. They proceeded to dig themselves in and surround the place with guns. I haven't seen these policemen yet, but I'm told that they are young, untrained and undisciplined. Pat seems to think that their arrival is the result of this wounded chap turning up, but I think it's more likely linked to the activity of the bandits in the area. In retrospect, it was probably best that I wasn't around when the injured man arrived because I may have been tempted to treat him, causing greater complications all round.

With all this on my mind, my head already buzzing with holiday memories, I tried to get a night's sleep. The following morning I got back to work, spending the day getting to know the new patients on the ward. After such a stupendous holiday in Nepal, I was feeling full of enthusiasm and happier than ever, despite all the latest problems in the hospital, surgical and political.

One of the pleasures of going away, of course, is the large pile of post waiting to be read on one's return, eight letters on this occasion! Once again, I write to say how grateful we are for the many packets of soup and Angel Delights that you send. The weather is becoming increasingly hot and sticky each day and we're looking forward to the beginning of the monsoon next month to bring the cooler breezes again. The school children have been using my bungalow today for their examination, so there are books and benches and bottles of ink all over the place. I do hope that you can read my writing as it's getting dark now and it's difficult to see.

20 May

Problems with Maggots

I'm settling down again after the holiday. We are enjoying strong fresh winds from the northwest which relieve the heat. It's so humid in the theatre by 8.30 a.m. that, after only one operation, I need a complete change of clothes and a bucket of water thrown over me! The number of outpatients has dropped off noticeably, due either to the seasonal change or to the harvesting of the crops, but it is a Godsend for us, as it allows us to concentrate on other aspects of the work, such as community and preventive health. Since I arrived back less than a fortnight ago, I've done eight tubal ligations and numerous D&Cs.

I saw an old lady with a nose-full of maggots yesterday! I have no idea how the condition had come about. It was a long and complicated job to clear her nostril as they were deeply embedded quite far back. As you can imagine, she was hugely grateful. We see maggot-infested wounds from time to time, but one reads that they don't seem to do much harm, rather the opposite, by aiding the healing of the lesion.

I'm sitting on the back veranda looking across to the green and brown ploughed fields on the other side of the river. The water is quite still this evening and looks like the Avon at Stratford. Having had a pleasant hour playing badminton with the nurses, we all went down to the river which they do several times a day. I was intending just to paddle, but the nurses took great pleasure in soaking me, the inevitable consequence of which was that I was compelled to have a swim, there and then, in my shirt and trousers. Indeed, it was cool and refreshing!

Yesterday we were invited to another village wedding feast. The invitation comes early in the day. Then you wait until dark and finally someone comes along with the message, "*Ekhan shob prostut.*" (All is now ready.) I think I've also mentioned before how all the beggars get invited too. Life is wonderful here in Bollobhpur and we share many blessings, for the villagers seem to brim with happiness despite the widespread poverty.

Naomi's Funeral

Thank you once again for the *South Wales Argus* which everybody reads here, after which it is sent down to *Rotnapur* for Tom and Di. The weather is hot again and so it will remain for the rest of the year. I am soaking wet with perspiration for eighteen hours a day, despite up to three changes of clothes.

A sad little ceremony took place on Sunday. We lost Naomi, one of our baby orphans. She died of tuberculosis despite exceptional care from us all. The nurses were so fond of her. At the age of nine months she weighed only seven and a half pounds. I had tried every treatment and diet to save her, but in the end, we were all relieved that she went. She had suffered so much ill health and discomfort. On Sunday, under the midday sun, a sad procession made up of nine nurses plus Pat, Eryl and myself, walked from the hospital to the village cemetery. *Monju*, one of the senior nurses, carried the baby garlanded with flowers and covered in a white sheet which reflected the bright sunlight.

Lizzie and Eryl are going off for their holiday to South India where they will hopefully meet up with Benny, who is now working as a paediatrician in *Vellore*. Lizzie is also hoping to locate the house in *Ootacamund* where her father was born. He had always claimed that *his* father had built the Indian Railways! Eryl returns to England in mid-June. We will be sad to see her go. Living so closely together for all these months, we get to know one another well, and she has been a great companion and help.

29 May Thursday 9.30 a.m.

A Court Appearance, a Lightning Strike and Moses Appears on the Road

Well, here I am in *Meherpur* again, waiting to go to court to give evidence for my friend *Biku,* whose life was in the balance last August when he suffered serious internal injuries having been stabbed in the abdomen. How these cases drag on! Still, it gives me an opportunity to have a few hours' break after a rather eventful week. On Monday, a member of the household was dismissed for stealing hospital sheets (the fourth dismissal in three months). That same night my house was broken into and my wardrobe ransacked for money. Thankfully, I was sleeping in the big house. They stole my razor blades again! I was building up a nice little stock! Yesterday we heard that one of the orphans, a fourteen-year-old lad, who was doing well at school in *Barisal,* was struck by lightning in a Christian village not far away, dying instantly. To top it all, a psychotic gentleman walked out in front of the jeep on our way home last evening, raising his hand as if he were Moses holding back the Red Sea and refusing to budge! It took a while for several villagers to quieten him down and allow us to pass. It was really sad for the poor chap. His eyes were flashing and his beard was flowing, but we had to laugh! If you lose your sense of humour out here, it gets really hard.

Despite all this, I'm in the best of health and happiness. The pre-monsoon evening skies are with us again with their astonishing display of rainbow colours and there's a fresh wind keeping us from being poached in the intense heat and humidity. We've had one or two storms and the roads are cutting up already. *Driver* had some difficulty getting us here this morning, but it will be another few weeks before we can take to the boats. I'm about to start reading the story of Tchaikovsky and looking forward to it. But I must go now as I'm due to appear before the magistrate.

3 June

An anxious morning with a woman in labour difficulties and now it's a hot afternoon. Thank heavens, the lady has just delivered safely. When I arrived at the court last week, they said that the case would be adjourned yet again. This will be for the fourth time. No justice for *Biku*! I've finished that book about Tchaikovsky, written very shortly before his death. We have several cassettes here and I've been enjoying his sixth symphony. I've just been comparing the hospital admissions for the last six months with the same period last year. The number of births has dropped by fifty, proving that our family planning project is effective. Fewer babies in the family means more food for the rest of the children which is good because, since rice has recently soared in price, some families barely manage to have one meal of rice a day.

It's ghastly hot here and desperately sticky. Even the heat from the hurricane lamp on the table beside me is producing a sweat. It must be doing my skin good! It's really busy in the hospital and I saw a hundred and fifteen men in the clinic yesterday. A couple of policemen armed with rifles forced themselves into the front of the queue and wanted to be seen immediately. Not wishing to be intimidated by them and siding with the patients who had been queuing for hours, I insisted that the policemen should go round to the back of the queue (which was now numbering about fifty). They must have sloped off because I didn't see them again. There's been an increase in the number of outpatients again recently, which is all a bit confusing.

10 June

Searching for Walmington-on-Sea

We are lying outside on the steps trying to remain cool! Pat is frantically trying to tune the radio so that we can listen to *Dad's Army*, but the reception has been very poor these last few nights so it looks as though we're going to be disappointed; Radio Ceylon, America, Holland, everything except *Dad's Army*! We've had quite a busy day: this morning I operated on a man with a nasty perforated appendix. Tonight he is quite stable. Just as we were finishing the appendicectomy, a message came through about a *poati* in trouble in *Meherpur*. So after I'd changed my op-clothes (which were absolutely sodden with perspiration) and grabbed a quick lunch, I hopped into the Land Rover and went to see her. She'd produced her last baby twenty-two years ago and she was huge – at least seventeen stone. We managed to deliver her without trouble. The Muslim family were delighted and brought *mishtis* (sweets) which went down well with a cuppa, then an hour's rest and back to Bollobhpur for tea. As I write, Engelbert Humperdinck has just started singing *Eternally* on crackling Radio Ceylon!

17 June 6.00 p.m.

The condition of the soldier, whose perforated appendix I removed last week, is remarkably good and now, just seven days post-op, he is ready to go home. From my point of view, it would seem to be a miraculous recovery. Unfortunately, we have just admitted another acute abdomen – this time it's probably a perforated gastric ulcer. This gives me something else to be anxious about, although I am not as worried as I used to be.

I've just stitched up the head of a little girl who fell down a well! She had two nasty gashes but was incredibly good and hardly cried at all. We spend a lot of time reading any book that we can lay our hands on. At present I'm reading Hugh Walpole's *Vanessa*.

I've been enjoying the magazine about Edward VII that you kindly sent last week and couldn't put it down. I was delighted to find the name *"Christopher Strauli"* in the cast list of a recent TV production. We met in Stratford over successive summers in the sixties and watched several RSC productions together. He went on to become an actor and here he is playing Winston Churchill on television! Had my life gone in another direction, it might have been me! Looking back, I'm so glad I didn't follow an acting career because, despite all its attractions, nobody could be happier in the life and work that I am doing.

Celebrating My Birthday

My 30th birthday, being such a milestone, gave me pause for thought. The first thing that comes to mind is gratitude to God for my wonderful life so far. It's been so full of happiness, thanks to my family and home and all the encouragement and love I've received. And then to arrive here! Wherever God might direct me in the future, I will always know that I was here in the *right* place at the *right* time of my life.

Actually, it turned out to be quite a working birthday. I performed another fistula operation and a primiparous breech delivery was threatening problems all day. It could have become quite complicated, but she finally delivered in the evening without trouble and we were all relieved and grateful.

The nurses had entertained me with a huge plateful of sweet rice and bananas and Bengali tea at 5.00 p.m. I was really full to the brim, but they were really kind and hospitable. A nice supper of tinned ham and a glass of sherry (saved from a British High Commission offering) made a special birthday meal. It's awfully hot and sticky as we wait for the first rains, so after supper we sat out on the steps under the stars, listening to Alistair Cook's *Letter from America*.

A Well-deserved Award for Florence

Today we hear that Florence has been awarded the MBE! We are so pleased and proud. I also received a letter from her saying what a lovely time she'd had visiting you and what a delight it had been to hear the tapes that I'd sent home last year. It's getting quite dark now, and heavy rain clouds are filling the sky. Maybe there will be some rain tonight. There's a mumble of voices coming across the garden from the hospital and someone is playing the Bengali radio in the distance. *Shonda*, a little eighteen-month orphan is playing at my feet.

22 June Sunday

Rabies

Just a note to let you know that all is well. Someone is going into *Meherpur* tomorrow and so will be able to post my letter. The roads are cutting up badly, so we are rather isolated until the river rises sufficiently for boating. Never mind, we've had one or two long-awaited downpours to cool us all off. Lizzie has returned from South India fit and well, and I'm ready to get back to work.

We admitted a case of rabies yesterday – a poor mother of five who had been bitten by a dog two months ago. It was a terrible death: restlessness, agitation and the classic fear of water, the very mention of which would restart her spasms. She eventually passed into a coma and died the following day, an end which seemed to be a welcome release for her. We have sent for vaccines, both for ourselves and for the nurses, which should arrive in a day or so. We certainly see everything out here.

The village school has taken over my bungalow for the rainy season so I've moved into the big house. Actually, it's more convenient to be living closer to the hospital as I don't have to walk over from the bungalow when I'm called out in the middle of the night. The girls have given me a beautiful leather bound Revised Standard Version Bible for my birthday. It has a zip! They must have bought it in Calcutta when they were last there. I'm reading some beautiful passages from Isaiah at the moment.

6 July Sunday

Sunday afternoon again with a full, but quiet, hospital at the moment. The rains are coming more frequently this week with a heavy shower every afternoon, but things dry out very quickly and it's great to have the refreshing cool breeze which comes with the rain because it makes sleeping at night more comfortable.

8 July Tuesday

I must finish this letter before it gets too dark, as my hurricane lamp doesn't give much light for writing letters. It's been raining heavily for the past twenty-four hours, and I wonder whether we'll be able to get to *Meherpur* tomorrow where I can post it.

Thank goodness it's been a quiet weekend. My rabies injections have almost been completed without too much discomfort, but now I'm nursing a nasty boil elsewhere. There's plenty of sympathy around and I'm dosing myself with appropriate antibiotics. I'm sure I'll be fine again soon. The girls even gave me breakfast in bed and I feel all the better for it. What a climate for minor illnesses! My present discomfort gives me more sympathy for my patients! I can hear the rumble of thunder in the distance, which makes me think that there's more rain on the way – or is it the sound of *Mogul* frying fish in the kitchen?

Thursday

The Earth Moves
We had some fun yesterday trying to get the Land Rover started by pushing it across the compound. It had a flat battery. But since there was no gradient in any direction, we didn't have much success! That meant that we couldn't go to *Meherpur* unless we'd walked and that would have taken hours. So I've had my first day off in seven weeks, reading a new Alistair MacLean novel and sleeping and generally relaxing. Thankfully, there were no emergencies, so it was very pleasant.

The new nurses had their exam this morning after their first three months. They were extremely nervous, but I'm glad to say all four of them passed well. Another new experience took place this evening. Tom and Di and the baby were down here about an hour ago and we felt a significant earthquake lasting about two minutes. The bamboo scaffolding on the church tower looked as though it was gently swaying in the breeze – but there was *no* breeze! Pat says such tremors do occasionally happen without causing any damage, so there is nothing to worry about.

The Servants Dismissed

Four of the household staff are under suspicion of having pinched four hundred *takas* from Lizzie's wardrobe. This is the second time this year that one of them has stolen money. It was all very upsetting and emotional, especially for Pat who feels that after twenty years of working here in Bollobhpur there is no one that she can trust. They just do not seem to be able to tell the truth or resist stealing anything that they can find. It is a really sad affair since *Mogul* the cook has been working in the house for years. There were many tears. Despite all this domestic distress we have been reading Colossians 3.12-17 together and the passage has given us great hope and goals to strive for.

21 July Monday

I'm looking out from my room down to the river, where the water level has gone up remarkably quickly over the last few days. Large clumps of water hyacinth are floating by. They clog up the rivers, lakes and ponds north of us for much of the year. Although the roads have completely disappeared under a quagmire of mud, the river isn't high enough for boating yet. So for the next few weeks we'll be travelling to *Meherpur* by one of the world's slowest forms of transport – the bullock cart. It will take four hours to cover ten miles! Still, it should be restful, though very bumpy to say the least.

Fractures, Pulleys and Strings

I've just returned from setting a little boy's arm. His fracture was just above the elbow and it was a rather tricky one to manipulate under anaesthesia, but all was well and he'll probably go home tomorrow. Many patients present with fractured arms and legs, each of which has to be reduced and set in plaster. We've had one or two patients with fractured femurs, whose broken limb is elevated by means of a series of pulleys, strings and weights known as *Russell's traction*. They seem quite content in this contraption for many weeks, but the outcome is good.

Welcome Bottle of Moselle

Lizzie flew to *Dhaka* last week and brought back a bottle of Moselle, which accompanied an exceedingly small chicken shared between the four of us. The rain clouds parted long enough for us to sit out on the steps under the half moon and listen to *Dad's Army* on the crackling radio.

We hear that inflation is at a record high in England and that food prices have gone through the roof. How clearly I remember those last few weeks at home. It only seems a few months ago, but what experiences I've had since then!

I'm extremely sad to read from your letters that I now have two divorced brothers. I'm thinking of the distress that these last few months must have caused both to them and to you. In my Bible reading this morning, I found the words of St. Paul: "*…let it be so … for God has called us to peace.*"

27 July Sunday

A Nine Hour Round Trip in a Bullock Cart

Last Wednesday we went to *Meherpur* in a bullock cart leaving at dawn – four and a half hours to get there and four and a half coming back! Still, as usual, there were many people there waiting for us when we arrived, so it was a worthwhile trip. We arrived back in time for dinner and a special tin of lager! It's possible that the roads might dry out a little over the next few days, so next week's journey could be either by Land Rover or rowing boat, depending on the rain.

5 August Tuesday

I'm sitting out here on the front steps, drinking a cup of tea and looking at the night sky. The Milky Way stretches clearly from one horizon to the other and there are millions of stars. As I have mentioned before, we frequently see shooting stars and satellites crossing over. I'm lying on my front, as I've got a rather sore backside, having cycled to *Meherpur* today – ten miles both ways. I set off early this morning, down through the villages which line the river and got there in an hour and a half. It was the court case yet again, and having hung around the police offices and courtrooms for two and a half hours, we were told for the fifth time that the case would be adjourned. There is such a lack of justice in this country. The poor chap *Biku* was stabbed in the abdomen over a year ago and although he recovered from three operations (quite miraculously, I would say) it's quite appalling that he hasn't yet seen the culprits brought to justice.

Our hospital in *Meherpur* is supervised by a chap called *Omor.* He and his wife have six daughters! After a pleasant sleep, I started back on the bike at 5.00 p.m. What a beautiful journey along the river! I can't remember having been so impressed by the colours – a full river, the waving rice and the trees. Many people in the villages greeted me as I cycled passed and asked from where I had come from and to where I was heading. If you ask a Bengali which way you should be aiming for, he doesn't say left or right, but thrusts his chin forward, using it to point in the required direction and simply says *"oodike"* (that way)! It was a bit hot and sweaty and now I'm paying the price, but well worth the trip, although, from the point of view of justice, it was disappointing once again. Lizzie is sitting next to me reading *The Agony and the Ecstasy* (the novel based on the life of Michelangelo) and Pat is getting through her seventh cup of tea in an hour.

The weeks are beginning to pass very quickly and it's strange to think there are only three further months of work for me out here. Lizzie is going home in six weeks' time so that the team will then be reduced to three, having been eight when I arrived.

13 August Wednesday

I've just finished the Meherpur Clinic and am now waiting for lunch. I'm looking at a kingfisher sitting on the telegraph wires just like swallows do at home. As usual, the week has flown by and it doesn't seem more than a day or two since I wrote my last letter. We did a caesarean section last Wednesday night and mother and baby are doing well. Since then, I've had lots to contend with including compound fractures and torn tendons. Over the weekend we had the company of two doctors from a Japanese missionary society looking at this area of Bangladesh before sending out a lady doctor. They were delightful company and, although busy surgeons in Tokyo, they were humble enough to assist me in one or two of our own operations. I was so proud of all the nurses. It is wonderful that *Togor*, now our senior nurse, had the opportunity of assisting a prestigious professor and did excellently well. He was really kind and helpful and, of course, I learnt a great deal. They were charming guests and we were sad when they left.

I hope this letter includes a sunny photograph of us all, reassuring you that I'm in good shape and enjoying this wonderful life with presently no earthquakes, bandits, rabies, boils or runny noses to contend with.

17 August Sunday

Coup d'état

No doubt you are worried about the news about the *coup d'état* that took place in *Dhaka* two days ago. Well it was bound to come! It's been obvious for over a year that something like this would eventually happen. It was a relief that the predicted bloodshed didn't follow though. Today we hear that the new government seems to be in full control and the curfew has been lifted.

Please be assured that this change of government has not disturbed us one bit and whatever is happening in *Dhaka* has little effect in these remote villages. We were eating breakfast on Friday morning, when *Driver* came in and said that *Sheikh Mujib* and most of his family had been killed in a military takeover, so we grabbed the radio and listened to the endless announcements of his death and the formation of a new government. The day was quiet and there was an immediate restriction on people's movements, everyone being concerned as to what was going to happen next. The Bangladeshi radio was confusing and not straightforward. We were waiting for the BBC News at 6.00 p.m. to find out what really was happening! It's strange to think that we have to wait for the news from London to discover what's going on a hundred and fifty miles away!

Even the commandant of the police camp came up to the hospital to hear the latest news! The reaction of the people has been minimal. In fact, we ourselves seem to be expressing more sadness about the killing of such a good man as *Sheikh Mujib* than the villagers themselves! Today we hear that the curfew has been lifted and that the country is getting back to normal. Angela, a VSO from *Jessore*, arrived last week and was caught by the national curfew and remains with us.

People seldom talk about the 1971 war of independence. Florence recalled how she took a large group of orphans across the border into India and occasionally one hears stories of cruelty and bodies floating down the river. But the aftermath of the conflict is still evident in the widespread poverty and the massive refugee camps in India created as a result of the displacement of huge numbers of people across the border.

On Wednesday night, I did another caesarean section. It took most of the night and we finished with breakfast at 6.00 a.m.! Mother and baby are doing well – what a thrill for us all! The weather has been so pleasant lately that it's difficult to imagine that there is trouble in *Dhaka*. We had a great game of gin rummy in moonlight on the steps last night. I won!

P.S. I just thought that I would censor some of my sentences on the previous page, on the off-chance that someone might read the letter. Hence the scribblings out.

22 August

To *Meherpur* by Boat

Wednesday was grand. We left early by boat and now that the water hyacinth has all gone, we had a speedy journey to *Meherpur* taking only three and a half hours. As the sun came up, the breathtaking skies with their multitude of rainbow colours, the bright greens of the undergrowth, the rice fields stretching away into the distance, the coconut trees, the kingfishers flying up and down the river, were all indescribable. If only I could paint! The splash of the water against the sides of the boat, as the oarsman rhythmically repeated his strokes, is soporific. Life is very pleasant.

Returning in the late afternoon, with four lady patients for sterilizations on board, was even better. It was rather like a Mothers' Union outing with lots of good humour. Bengali people seem to be able to sit in one position for hours without moving in the tiny space, and the two newborn babies hardly made a sound.

26 August

No Shoes or Socks

All is well here and we have not been affected at all by the political crisis in *Dhaka*. The news is very scanty and we await the BBC News from London every evening, so you probably know as much as we do. Life continues as usual with a full ward and busy clinics. As I write, we have another eclamptic emergency going on and I rush out every half hour when a nurse shouts "*Fit!*" so I may not get to the end of this letter in one go. It has been exceptionally heavy and hot these last few days, but there's been no rain. We are wondering if the rains are over early this year because we don't relish an extra month of this awful humidity.

Lizzie is leaving in three weeks and is already quite sad about it. It will be such a break from all the friends she has made here. Still, I expect we'll have some farewell feasts before she goes and, as always, there will be a lot of fun mixed up with the sadness of parting. I wonder if you received my note about purchasing a ticket from Calcutta to London.

7.00 p.m.: The baby was safely delivered an hour ago. All is now well and peaceful in the ward. I've just had an early supper and am taking the opportunity to get this letter finished before we leave for *Meherpur* tomorrow morning by boat at the unearthly hour of 5.00 a.m. We usually have enough room to stretch our legs out, but tomorrow we're taking a few patients, one of them being the caesarean section lady of two weeks ago whom we brought back by boat in a desperate state the day before.

It just struck me that for my return in November may I ask you to bring a pair of socks and shoes to Heathrow. I haven't a pair of shoes to my name and haven't worn socks for two years – just flipflops.

3 September Wednesday 4.45 p.m.

No apparent disturbances here in *Meherpur* where the political trouble in *Dhaka* seems a long way off. We've had a busy day, seeing about two hundred and fifty patients between us this morning, followed by my giving an obstetric lecture to the nurses after lunch, the torrential rain pouring down outside our little lecture room as I was doing so. It's difficult to teach in Bengali, but the girls were patient and I hope that everything was understood in the end with lots of laughter and fun on the way.

9 September Tuesday 5.45 p.m.

Our Good Friend Takes an Overdose
I'm sitting here at my table drinking a glass of fresh coconut milk straight out of a coconut and writing by lamplight. There's still some light outside, although the nights are drawing in. Many thanks for all your lovely letters describing a wonderful summer at home, "*almost tropical*", someone has written in a letter I received today.

It's been a worrying day, but we have much to thank God for. The story started on Thursday. During my enormous men's clinic in the morning, someone stole a large amount of money from the dispensary tin. It turned out to be *Kolpona,* one of our best junior nurses, a long gangly girl with a characteristic giggle, very bright and helpful. We were so sad and disappointed because this was the third time that cash had been stolen by the staff in the last few months. *Kolpona* was discovered with the money and having confessed, got a very loving and understanding telling off by Pat. However, shame in this part of the world comes not from 'doing something wrong', but from 'being found out'. The *lajja* was too much for the poor girl and she took an overdose of phenobarbitone in the early hours of Monday morning. Many people, especially young women, attempt suicide and are frequently successful.

Kolpona, a good and happy person with whom I've worked alongside almost every day for two years was admitted in a deep coma. At 6.00 a.m. this morning she went into respiratory failure with an irregular pulse. Having intubated her, we manually respirated her with an Ambu bag for eight hours in the hope that spontaneous breathing would return. It was a very worrying time for us all and an overwhelming sense of responsibility for me since she was one of the Bollobhpur 'family'. All we could do was pray and, at 2.00 p.m., she began breathing by herself again, at first little breaths, then deeper and deeper, until regular respirations were re-established. Now she is in a light coma and her blood pressure and pulse are satisfactory. The Lord heard our prayers!

Oh, what happiness and joy, both spiritual and professional, that each day brings! How happy these few years have been and I shall leave Bollobhpur with mixed feelings; the multitudes of friends I have made and the wonderful things God has allowed me to see! But I'm quite sure the Lord has more work for me to do in England and I'm being called back to serve Him there.

10 September Wednesday 8.50 a.m.

I'm finishing this letter on the boat. We've already been on the river for two and a half hours and we are now approaching the outskirts of

Meherpur. I hope there won't be too many people at the outpatients because I want to do a vasectomy before we set off home, perhaps by three or four this afternoon.

16 September Tuesday 2.00 p.m.

Kolpona did not regain consciousness and died a few days later, despite our efforts. We were all shocked and sad and I still can't believe it. We tried hard to move on, for the week had been planned for Lizzie's farewell feasts and picnics. We spent the whole of Sunday with the nurses. They took us on a boat with a sack of rice, vegetables and mutton for a curry, which was to be cooked on the bank further down the river. Lizzie, as the special guest, was given the privilege of mixing the oil, meat and spices with her right hand. The week which started so tragically ended on a happier note with much laughter and fun.

Thursday 8.30 p.m.

It's sad and quiet here today. Lizzie left Bollobhpur yesterday with the hospital and domestic staff on the steps waving her a weepy goodbye. Pat got her visa at the very last minute, so they could both visit the Taj Mahal in Delhi before returning to Calcutta from where Lizzie will fly home.

23 September

Thoughts of Returning Home
My busy work continues with much satisfaction and delight, many an evening is spent with my head deep in books. Last week we wondered whether we might have had a cholera epidemic on our hands, but, after admitting five severely dehydrated patients with gastroenteritis, the potential outbreak seems to have disappeared. The hospital is running smoothly, despite the fact that there are now only two of us left. Now that the girls have gone, I'm learning new

jobs, such as making up bitter tasting cough mixtures from their basic ingredients. Despite the awful taste, they are extremely popular and much appreciated by the patients.

Words cannot express the sense of fulfilment that these last two years have brought me. I am approaching the date of my departure with mixed feelings – on the one hand, I'm so much looking forward to seeing you all again, yet, on the other, there is a resistance to let go of my work here and the relationships that I have made. The emotional hurly-burly of joys and disappointments, moments of peace followed by hours of hectic activity, is draining, but I wouldn't have missed a minute of it.

I am reminded of the story of the healed demoniac who sat at Jesus's feet and wanted to stay with him. "*Go home,*" Jesus said, "*and tell your friends what God has done.*"

I discovered an old library book here called *Noël Coward*. It was crammed with photographs of Gertrude Lawrence, John Gielgud and other famous names and, as you can guess, I could barely put it down.

Last week was great fun too. I was clambering into the boat after a long day at *Meherpur* and lost my footing and fell into the river! I got soaking wet, despite the fact that it was only three foot deep. Everyone was roaring with laughter including the boatman! I was laughing too!

29 September Sunday 5.00 p.m.

Well, it looks ever more certain that I'll be arriving at Heathrow on Monday 17 November as planned, although experience tells me it could be earlier or later. I'm awaiting the arrival of an open ticket from London. It certainly won't take long to pack up my things, I've got so little in the way of belongings. I'm going to Calcutta to spend a few days with my good friends at the Oxford Mission Fathers in *Behala*, then a flight on Sunday night will bring me home again! Isn't God wonderful! Here is a man who has experienced life in all its extremities, who has seen far more of his patients die than he would have wished, but who has known the strength and goodness of God in his own life and in the lives of others! I fear the enormous culture shock as I re-adjust to the different values and priorities of the West.

8 October

Cholera Outbreak

I mentioned in my letter the emergence of an outbreak of a cholera-type illness. We thought it would be short-lived, but now it is affecting the whole local area. We are admitting increasing numbers of severely dehydrated patients of all ages with vomiting and diarrhoea and it is hard to keep up with the constant need to put up drips for their rehydration. Such is the limited number of infusion sets that we have to sharpen the intravenous needles on emery paper and re-sterilize the giving-sets between patients. However, the patients seem to recover fairly quickly after they have been rehydrated. When they are discharged others are admitted. It's been a really busy week, so I was glad to get back to the house from time to time to take a break. The weather is a little cooler, which makes a pleasant change, a sheet now being required occasionally in the early morning.

Totting up the Figures

I've been looking at the admissions over the last two years and it's quite interesting to note that we admitted one hundred tetanus patients: fifty of them were neonates, twenty-seven were children and twenty-three were adults. The overall mortality rate was 51%.

I have performed over two hundred and fifty tubal ligations and countless other operations.

With regards to obstetrics: of the five hundred and fifty-two deliveries, a hundred and fourteen presented with complications requiring intervention. Sadly, we recorded forty-seven stillbirths and thirteen maternal deaths, a far greater mortality rate than we would have wished, but many of these unfortunate women were admitted '*in extremis*' presenting with complications that are rarely, if ever, seen at home and we did everything we could to save them.

19 October Sunday 1.00 p.m.

This afternoon at 4.00 p.m., I've been asked to be the godfather of the two-month-old baby brother of *Monju*, one of the nurses. They asked me to name the little chap. A Bible name is important, so I was pleased to name him Mark, after our own Mark. I'm so glad to be able to keep a special link with at least one little Bengali child out of all the scores of children who have become my friends, though I don't see quite so much of my little village pals since I have moved to the big house.

I spent a few wet days in *Dhaka*, saying goodbye to several friends, doing a little shopping and meeting the young doctor from the Royal Gwent whom we thought might have replaced me here. But it was not to be, for he was the answer to someone else's need and is soon moving to the refugee camps where he will certainly need our prayers for the huge job that lies ahead of him. Bishop James Blair is retiring soon and has been attending farewell ceremonies all over the country. He is an exceedingly kind gentleman and has always been pleasant to me. It was good to have the opportunity to say goodbye to him and to Keith and Ruby who came out to Bangladesh with me. As Diocesan administrators they've had a tough time living in a really ghastly part of *Old Dhaka*, beleaguered by the inefficiency of everything bureaucratic over here.

I visited a hospital while I was there and had a chuckle when I saw a notice on the wall of one of the wards, written in Bengali and English – "*DON'T SPIT SCATTEREDLY!*"

I'd better finish this letter because the boat is about to depart with the post. How strange that, from a distance across the river, I can hear a Bengali version of *Those were the days my friend*, and I'm reminded of Mary Hopkin.

28 October

Home Soon
I'm writing to you by lamplight, although it's only 5.30 p.m., but the nights are drawing in again. There seem to be lots of odds and ends

for me to do including clearing out my cupboard before I deliver an obstetric lecture to the nurses. I'm anxious to complete the course I'm giving, but it's going to be a bit of a rush.

10.00 p.m.: The lecture went well. We have three volunteer engineers staying with us and we enjoyed supper together this evening as they told us about their work, so different from surgery and obstetrics. I'd better get some sleep now as we've got the Meherpur Clinic in the morning and innumerable patients who will be waiting for us when we arrive.

4 November Tuesday

Do Not Fear the Lions
Looking back over these last two amazing years and how each new obstetric, surgical and medical crisis has had to be dealt with, cases often lying far outside my previous training or experience, I am reminded of that encouraging passage from Bunyan's *The Pilgrim's Progress*. As the hero, Christian, approaches the Palace Beautiful with hopes of getting lodging for the night, he sees two roaring lions which test his faith and stop him from going further. At the palace gate, there is a porter whose name is "Watchful" who reassures him with the words: *"Do not fear the lions, for they are chained."*

Well this will be the last letter I will be writing to you from Bollobhpur! I'm settling down to write to you with a hurricane lamp and a brass vase of red flowers in front of me. The temperature has now dropped in the evening and morning. On Saturday, I used a sheet for the first time and this evening I'll have a blanket nearby just in case.

Saying Goodbye to Good Friends
I've already been invited to several farewell meals. Last week we ate in a Muslim village not far away, at the home of a little boy whose legs I grafted after a nasty accident. On Sunday we were in a tiny Christian village at the home of a young girl who needed a caesarean section. Today we were at the house of *Biku*, my old friend, on whom

we operated three times after bandits had stabbed him last year. Many old patients have come up to the hospital to say goodbye, including *Jotin* whose legs I amputated eighteen months ago. He was so grateful for what I had done to remove his pain. He was whizzing around on a homemade bogey cart, propelling himself with his padded hands. It's been wonderful to stay connected with them all. On Thursday and Friday we will eat rice meals in the village homes of the nurses; on Saturday we will be at the orphanage and on Sunday we will enjoy a feast on the veranda of the nurses' home. So I will have put on some weight by the time you meet me. I am also trying to finish the lectures with the girls, even if it means doing so on the evening before my departure. It's great fun because the more involved I get in the subject, the worse my Bengali becomes!

I've started giving away my spare old clothes, a shirt to old *Simon*, my regular leprosy patient, a pullover to *Bimal Mallick* whom I met in the freezing cold last winter, stopping in the middle of the road to give thanks to God under the stars. He is a great man of prayer and it's such a pleasure to give away even these old things to such villagers as himself and others.

I thank God that I've been given the opportunity to spend two wonderful years here at Bollobhpur and now I'm looking forward, with much excitement, to stepping off the plane and seeing you all. I arrive at Heathrow at 8.25 a.m. on the 7th of November.

POSTSCRIPT

Florence returned to England and married at the age of sixty-two. She travelled regularly to Tower Hamlets in London to act as an interpreter for Bengali families. In 1976 she was the subject of Thames Television's *This Is Your Life*. Among the many friends who surprised her that night was *Driver*, who had been especially flown over from Bangladesh to appear on the programme.

Pat retired to Bristol and became a district nurse. She raised several thousands of pounds for Bollobhpur Hospital and provided friendship, support and accommodation for many young people via the Bristol International Students' Centre.

Meg returned to England to work as a health visitor amongst the Bengali community in London's East End. In 1983 she married John, whom she had met in a refugee camp in North Bengal. After twelve years as programme organiser for the BBC Bengali service, John, supported by Meg, returned to Methodist Ministry amongst the Caribbean community in Hackney.

Becky completed her nursing and midwifery training in England and shortly afterwards returned to Bangladesh to work amongst village midwives and health workers. She later resumed her career in London, working in training, development and management roles for the NHS.

Benny continued his career at the Christian Medical College, *Vellore*, Tamil Nadu. In 1974 he gained an FRCP in Edinburgh and went on to become a leading paediatrician and child specialist in *Chennai*, India.

Eryl worked as a health visitor, but soon offered herself for overseas service once again, this time in Malaysia. After eight further years abroad, she accepted a senior NHS Management role in the South of England and worked there until she retired.

Tom and Dianne completed twelve years in *Rotnapur* and returned to Durham Diocese where they continued in Parish Ministry until their retirement. Alongside his love of motorbikes, Tom became a well-known local artist. His supply of Burmese cheroots eventually ran out.

Bryan continued to travel, marketing heavy machinery to all four corners of the world, finally specialising in the developing technology of wind turbines.

* * *

Julian and Lizzie married in 1977! They have three children, who can't quite believe that their parents experienced so many adventures when they were young! Lizzie became increasingly involved in the Fairtrade Movement which took her to many projects across the continents. She became a leading agent for Traidcraft in the UK.

Julian worked as a family doctor in the Midlands for twenty-nine years. Shortly after his return from Bangladesh he became an Anglican priest and, with the help of Lizzie, successfully combined the two vocations. He celebrated forty years of active ministry in 2021, and still tells stories of those memorable days in Bollobhpur.